Irene C. Fountas & Gay Su Pinnell

Sing a Song of
Poetry

Irene C. Fountas & Gay Su Pinnell

Sing a Song of
Poetry

A Teaching Resource for Phonemic Awareness, Phonics, and Fluency

Grade 2

Revised Edition

HEINEMANN
Portsmouth, NH

Heinemann
361 Hanover Street
Portsmouth, NH 03801–3912
www.heinemann.com

Offices and agents throughout the world

Cataloging-in-Publication Data is on file at the Library of Congress.

ISBN-13: 978-0-325-09916-3

Previously published under:
ISBN-13: 978-0-325-10552-9
ISBN 0-325-00657-1
978-0-325-00657-4

Editorial: Kimberly Capriola, David Pence
Production: Laurie Peyser
Cover and interior designs: Monica Ann Crigler
Typesetter: Gina Poirier Design
Manufacturing: Erin St. Hilaire

Printed in the United States of America on acid-free paper
22 21 20 19 18 VP 1 2 3 4 5

Contents

Poems

Contents

E

F

G

H

I

Contents

N

O

P

Q

R

W

Introduction

Sing a Song of Poetry rolls off the tongue and moves the heart and spirit, if not the feet and hands. Rhythmical language of any sort delights young children as it surrounds them with the magical sounds of dancing words. But poetry, verse, and song provide the magic of teaching as well; indeed, oral language is the doorway to the world of written language and the foundation for literacy. As second graders respond to the sound patterns, intriguing words, and inspiring ideas they find in poems, songs, and rhymes, they are learning invaluable lessons about the ways in which our language works—knowledge that will serve them well as they become readers and writers.

The poems, songs, and rhymes in this volume are a rich source of language, ideas, and imagery that will help second graders use and enjoy oral and written language. This volume is a companion to *Fountas & Pinnell Phonics, Spelling, and Word Study Lessons, Grade 2* (2019). It can also be used as a stand-alone resource for language and literacy opportunities in any early childhood or primary classroom.

Elephant

The elephant carries a great big trunk.
She never packs it with her clothes.
It has no lock and it has no key,
But she takes it wherever she goes.

A *Sing a Song of Poetry, Grade 2* poem cut out and pasted into a personal poetry book then illustrated by a second grader.

Experiences with poetry help children become aware of the phonological system of language and provide a foundation for matching sounds with letters, letter clusters, and word parts. You can use poems, songs, and rhymes to

- help children listen for and identify rhyming words;
- help children connect words that have the same beginning, ending, or medial sound;
- combine sounds to form words and check with the letters;
- match sounds to letters in words;
- help children divide words into separate sounds and match to letters;
- familiarize children with onomatopoetic words;
- introduce the culture, traditional language, and rhythmic patterns of nursery rhymes;
- draw attention to synonyms and antonyms;
- stimulate and enrich language development;

- develop word-solving strategies by helping them notice words; syllables; rhymes; onsets and rimes; and beginning, ending, and medial sounds;
- enhance oral language use in articulate ways;
- instill an appreciation of poetry and prose;
- build vocabulary;
- help children participate in fluent, phrased reading;
- encourage children to use intonation to reflect meaning;
- develop meaningful concepts about print (words, word parts, punctuation);
- help children explore writing; and
- draw attention to a variety of verbs and adjectives.

Once a poem is introduced in your classroom, it has multiple uses for teaching. Below are some examples.

- Reread the poem to have children highlight rhyming words with highlighter tape.
- Have children find and take apart compound words.
- Reread the poem with sticky notes over rhyming words so children can predict.
- Cover all but the first letter of several words, and have children predict and then check them as you reread.
- Have children highlight any features of words that they are studying: e.g., consonant clusters, onsets, rimes, and endings.
- Have children highlight base words, prefixes, and suffixes.
- Cover names in the poem with sticky notes and substitute with children's names.
- Give children a small version of the poem that they can glue in a personal poetry book and then illustrate.
- During independent work time, let children read their personal poetry book with a partner.
- During independent work time, children can read the chart with a partner.

In addition to activities like those above, read the suggestions in small print at the bottom of each poem. They describe ways you can work with the poem—sometimes adding verses or changing them.

Children love poetry with rhythm and rhyme; the language of poetry sings inside their heads. As they grow in experience, they also learn to appreciate poetry without rhyme, as well as the sensory images and unique perspectives it evokes. Poetry is related to the many cultures from which children come; by sharing cultures, they construct the common experiences of childhood.

Poetry provides resources for the heart and spirit. Immersing children in poetry at an early age instills a lifelong habit of enjoying language and seeking out poetry in order to expand our vision. Poetry joins us to the past and to our fellow human beings in the present.

Values and Goals of Poetry in Second-grade Classrooms

Poetry expands children's oral language abilities as it:
- builds a repertoire of the unique patterns and forms of language;
- helps children become sensitive to and enjoy the sounds of language—rhymes, alliteration, assonance, onomatopoeia (*buzz, whiz, woof*);
- supports articulation and elocution;
- extends listening and speaking vocabularies;
- expands knowledge of the complex syntax of language;
- encourages children to manipulate and play with language;
- develops understanding of complex letter-sound relationships;
- makes it easy for children to isolate and identify sounds, take words apart, and change sounds in words to make new words; and
- provides rich examples of comparisons such as similes and metaphors.

Poetry expands children's written language abilities as it:
- introduces more complex vocabulary in a meaningful context;
- expands oral vocabulary which fuels variety in word choice;
- provides opportunities to notice spelling patterns;
- provides experience with varied and complex syntax;
- provides a supported situation within which they can learn more high-frequency words;
- provides examples of different kinds of words—compound words, base words, contractions, plurals, words with suffixes and/or prefixes, homophones, homographs, synonyms, and antonyms; and
- provides the opportunity to participate in fluent, phrased reading.

Poetry expands children's content knowledge as it:
- provides new perceptions and ideas for them to think about;
- helps them develop conceptual understandings;
- encourages them to develop a sense of humor; and
- sensitizes them to the forms and styles of poetry.

Poetry contributes to children's social knowledge and skills as it:
- provides artistic and aesthetic experiences;
- promotes a sense of community through an enjoyment of shared reading;
- gives them access to English-speaking culture;
- provides a window to many other cultures;
- provides a common language for a group of children to share; and
- creates memories of shared enjoyable times.

The Language and Literary Features of Poetry

The following unique elements provide the essence of poetry's appeal. In the poems appropriate for young children, language patterns, rhyme, rhythm, and humor dominate, but all the elements are present.

Rhyme

Many of the simple poems that children enjoy include words that rhyme. Rhyme is the repetition of the last vowel and consonant sounds in words in verse, especially at the ends of lines. For example, in the poem "The Months of the Year," the words *showers* and *gillyflowers* rhyme because the sounds after /sh/ in *showers* are repeated in the third and fourth syllables of *gillyflowers*.

In this book, most of the rhyming words have one or two syllables. To understand rhyme in one-syllable words, it's helpful to understand the parts of a syllable. In a syllable, the onset is the part (the consonant, consonant cluster, or consonant digraph) that comes before the vowel. In a syllable, the rime is the ending part containing the letters that represent the vowel sound and the consonant letters that follow. For example, in the one-syllable word *play*, the onset is *pl* and the rime is *ay*. In the word *day*, the onset is *d* and the rime is *ay*. The words *play* and *day* rhyme because they have rimes that sound the same. Remember, two rimes with different spellings (such as *may* and *sleigh*) can rhyme if they have the same sounds.

Consider the the first stanza from Edward Lear's "Calico Pie":

> Calico pie,
>
> The little birds fly
>
> Down to the calico tree.
>
> Their wings were blue,
>
> And they sang "Tilly-loo!"
>
> Till away they flew;
>
> And they never came back to me!
>
> They never came back,
>
> They never came back,
>
> They never came back to me!

The words *pie* and *fly* rhyme. Likewise, the words *blue* and *flew* rhyme. Rhyme is appealing and memorable; rhyme always refers to the sound of the ending part of the word, not necessarily the spelling.

Rhythm

The beat, or *rhythm*, of poetry brings delight to children as they chant rhymes and songs in unison. Both rhyme and rhythm make it easy for them to recite, remember, and (after one or two shared readings) read poems independently.

For example, consider the poem "Stepping Stones":

> Stepping over stepping stones, one, two, three,
>
> Stepping over stepping stones, come with me.
>
> The river's very fast,
>
> And the river's very wide,
>
> And we'll step across on stepping stones
>
> And reach the other side.

Figurative and Archaic Language

As young children internalize poetry, they respond to the sensory images and figurative language. Poetry often uses language that compares two objects or ideas to allow the reader to see something more clearly or understand something in a new way, as in the poem "Jack Frost":

> Jack Frost bites your nose.
>
> He chills your cheeks and freezes your toes.
>
> He comes every year when winter is here
>
> And stays until spring is near.

Another example is from Sara Coleridge's "The Months of the Year":

> March brings breezes loud and shrill,
>
> Stirs the dancing daffodil.

Often rhymes, chants, and songs contain *onomatopoeia*, which is the representation of sound with words. For example, words like *whoosh* sound like the phenomenon they represent. Consider this example from "A Thunderstorm":

> Boom, bang, boom, bang,
>
> Rumpety, lumpety, bump!
>
> Zoom, zam, zoom, zam,
>
> Clippity, clappity, clump!
>
> Rustles and bustles
>
> And swishes and zings!
>
> What wonderful sounds
>
> A thunderstorm brings.

Poetry often presents children with verses that have been enjoyed for centuries. Sometimes they can internalize archaic language like *porridge* and *candlestick* as they chant and sing. But some archaic concepts may warrant explanation: e.g., the concept of courting as well as riding with a sword and scabbard like in the poem "Frog Went A-Courtin'." Additionally, old-fashioned language structures and expressions like *pray tell it me* and *hark the bell* in the poem "Higgledy, Piggledy, See How They Run," a *petticoat* in "Daffy Down Dilly," or the word *nought* in "Some One" may need to be defined. They are often—though not solely—present in nursery rhymes.

Language Patterns

Rhymes and poems are enjoyable in large part because of the language patterns that are included. *Alliteration*, the repetition of consonant sounds, is evident in the tongue twister "One Old Oxford Ox":

> One old Oxford ox opening oysters.
>
> Two toads totally tired trying to trot to Tisbury.
>
> Three thick thumping tigers taking toast for tea.
>
> Four finicky fishermen fishing for funny fish.
>
> Five frippery Frenchmen foolishly fishing for frogs.
>
> Six sportsmen shooting snipe.
>
> Seven Severn salmon swallowing shrimp.
>
> Eight eminent Englishmen eagerly examining England.
>
> Nine nibbling noblemen nibbling nectarines.
>
> Ten tinkering tinkers tinkering ten tin tinderboxes.
>
> Eleven elephants elegantly equipped.
>
> Twelve typographical topographers typically translating types.

Children love these tongue twisters, and they are an excellent way to help them internalize initial sounds. Another good example is the poem "She Sells Seashells":

> She sells seashells
>
> On the seashore.
>
> The shells that she sells
>
> Are seashells I'm sure.
>
> So if she sells seashells
>
> On the seashore,
>
> I'm sure that the shells
>
> Are seashore shells.

Another common pattern is the repetition of vowel sounds, called *assonance*. For example, the poem "Moses Supposes":

> Moses supposes his toeses are roses,
>
> But Moses supposes erroneously;
>
> For nobody's toeses are posies of roses,
>
> As Moses supposes his toeses to be.

Repetition

Many poems, particularly songs, have repeating stanzas or phrases. Notice that in the first two stanzas of the following poem, "Aiken Drum," the phrases [*There was a man*] *lived in the moon*, [*And he played upon*] *a ladle*, and *And his name was Aiken Drum* are repeated.

> There was a man lived in the moon,
>
> Lived in the moon, lived in the moon.
>
> There was a man lived in the moon,
>
> And his name was Aiken Drum.
>
> *Chorus*
> > *And he played upon a ladle,*
> >
> > *A ladle, a ladle,*
> >
> > *He played upon a ladle,*
> >
> > *And his name was Aiken Drum.*

Rhythmic repetition like this helps children learn these rhymes easily; many have been set to music and can be sung, such as the poem "Ive Been Working on the Railroad."

Sensory Images

Poetry arouses the senses. Just a few words can evoke memories, elicit visual images, point out absurdities, and help us enter unique worlds. Such poems often center on nature. They offer figurative language that appeals to the five senses and enriches children's own language. An example is the poem, "Who Has Seen the Wind?" by Christina Rossetti:

Who has seen the wind?

Neither I nor you:

But when the leaves hang trembling

The wind is passing through.

Who has seen the wind?

Neither you nor I:

But when the trees bow down their heads

The wind is passing by.

Important Areas of Learning for Second Graders

An important benefit of using poetry in second-grade classrooms is the facilitation of oral language development. Through their involvement in poetry, children expand their knowledge of the vocabulary and syntax of English as well as their sensitivity to the *phonology,* or sounds of the language. In addition, using poetry has profound implications for helping children learn to read and write. See *Guided Reading: Responsive Teaching Across the Grades*, Second Edition (Fountas and Pinnell 2017) and *Word Matters: Teaching Phonics and Spelling in the Reading/ Writing Classroom* (Pinnell and Fountas 1998).

Several important areas of learning form a foundation for becoming literate. Even though formal reading instruction began in the second half of kindergarten, children need to continue developing along all of these dimensions throughout the early childhood years.

Letter-Sound Relationships

The phonological system encompasses the sounds of a language. When children hear, chant, or sing poems, they become more aware of sound patterns and how they are connected (for example, words that rhyme or words that start the same).

Gradually, they are able to identify the individual sounds (or *phonemes*) in words. *Phonemic awareness,* or the ability to identify individual sounds in words, is essential when children are learning to connect sounds and letters. Most second graders are aware of phonemes, but they are still learning the relationships between complex spelling patterns as they reflect sounds. Children need to play with language and manipulate sounds. They can

- listen for and identify rhyming words;
- listen for and identify syllables within words;
- listen for and identify onsets and rimes;
- listen for individual sounds in words;
- match words with similar sounds;
- break words into individual sounds (phonemes) and into syllables;
- blend sounds to form words;
- match sounds and letters; and
- match sounds with complex letter patterns.

To be able to recognize letters, children need to distinguish the features that make one letter different from every other letter, and most second graders have full control of the alphabet. They are, however, still learning the patterns of letters as they appear in words so that they can use larger units for efficient decoding. In poetry, children will meet a larger variety. Moreover, these words are laid out in ways that make it easy for readers to see connections. Through repeated exposure to letters in the poems they experience in shared reading, children begin to notice the letters that are embedded in print. They can

- notice and locate letters patterns in words;
- connect words with similar patterns; and
- solve words by using context of rhyme.

Book and Print Features

Encounters with poetry help younger children understand the connections of print and how it "works." For second graders, a poem offers a format that is very important for the communication of meaning. The layout also guides the voice. Children can

- notice poetry as the conveyor of intense meaning in a concise way;
- notice line breaks and reflect them with the voice; and
- notice and use punctuation.

Fluency

Second graders will enjoy the feeling of fluency phrasing and intonation of the language. Supported by the group, they can read more complex syntax than they usually encounter. Children can

- read in phrases;
- use expression;
- reflect punctuation;
- use phrasing to reflect meaning;
- vary intonation and stress to reflect meaning; and
- read with enthusiasm.

Selecting Poetry

Selecting poetry for children depends on your purpose. Remember that children listen to and recite more complex poems than they can read at first. Knowing poems, songs, and rhymes increases their ability to notice the sounds of language; they learn many new words to add to their oral vocabulary. When they repeat familiar poems, they are using the syntax, or grammar, of written language, which is different from their everyday speech. Experiencing and internalizing this complex language sets the scene for reading and understanding the texts they read independently. Poems that second graders like may show features like

- humor;
- exaggeration;
- silly situations;
- rhyme and rhythm;
- riddles; and
- sensory images.

The poems in this book represent a gradient of difficulty. At the beginning of the year, select simpler poems, and then gradually increase the level of challenge. The poems in the chart below illustrate a continuum of difficulty.

1. Simplest

Gold Ships

There are gold ships.

There are silver ships.

But there's no ship

Like a friendship.

2. More Difficult

The Ptarmigan

The ptarmigan is strange,

As strange as he can be;

Never sits on the ptelephone poles

Or roosts upon a ptree.

And the way he ptakes pto spelling

Is the strangest thing pto me.

3. Most Difficult

December Leaves

The fallen leaves are cornflakes

That fill the lawn's wide dish,

And night and noon

The wind's a spoon

That stirs them with a swish.

The sky's a silver sifter,

A-sifting white and slow,

That gently shakes

On crisp brown flakes

The sugar known as snow.

Verse 1 is simple and short. There are few syllables, there is repetition, and there is a little play with the meaning and use of the word *ship*. Verse 2 is slightly longer than the first. It uses playful spellings to show how words like *ptarmigan* can sound different than they look because of one or more silent letters. Verse 3, "December Leaves" by Kaye Starbird, is the longest in length, and its metaphoric imagery demands more of the reader. Of the three selections, only number three has real poetic quality. The others are verses children will enjoy in a way that also helps them to appreciate poetry.

As you select poems to share, consider your children's previous experience, skill with language, and vocabulary. If you begin with easy poems and they learn them very quickly (for example, they join in during shared reading), provide slightly more complex examples.

Planning for Teaching Opportunities When Revisiting a Text

As short texts, poems provide a multitude of opportunities for learning about language. Sharing poetry will give children plenty of chances to:

- use interesting language;
- say and connect words of one, two, and three or more syllables;
- say and connect words that rhyme or that begin alike;
- say words, noticing beginning and ending sounds of consonants and consonant clusters;
- say words, noticing vowel sounds and vowel patterns;
- notice base words and affixes (prefixes and suffixes);
- make comparisons;
- notice figurative language; and
- notice synonyms, antonyms, and homophones.

After enjoying a poem several times, you may want to revisit the text with children to help them notice aspects of words or language patterns. The following grid helps you think about the varied opportunities in some sample texts. In each box, we list possible features that children can notice within a poem. You can try planning some poems out for yourself in advance or use the blank grid to keep a record of your teaching points within each poem as you make them.

WORD-ANALYSIS TEACHING OPPORTUNITIES WHEN REVISITING POETRY

Title	Type of Text (e.g., limerick, tongue twister, couplet, free verse)	Phonogram Patterns (e.g., -ack, -ome, -eep, -own)	Letter-Sound (e.g., beginning or ending consonants, consonant clusters, and consonant digraphs)	High-Frequency Words	Other (e.g., concept words; homonyms; metaphors and similes; names; new vocabulary; plurals; rhyming words; syllables)
At the Seaside	3-line verses 3 sets of rhyming words	-en, -own, -ide, -ood, -ade, -ave, -ig, -and, -ore, -ole, -ike, -up, -ame, -ill, -ome	Beginning *wh, wd, b, th, s, sp, g, t, m, sh, h, l, c, n* Ending *n, s, d, v, g, r, k, p, l, m, t, d*	*when, I, was, down, the, a, they, to, me, my, like, in, every, came, up, it, could, come, no*	simile (*empty like a cup*), new vocabulary word (*spade*), rhyming words (e.g., *sea, me*), two-syllable words (*sandy, empty, every*), compound word (*beside*)
Betty Botter	rhythmic, alliterative tongue twister	-ome, -ut, -aid, -ut, -at, -ill, -ake, -it, -et, -an	Beginning *b, s, sh, th, p, m, w, h, tw* Ending *r, t, m, d, s, f, n, l, k*	*some, but, she, said, this, if, I, put, it, in, my, will, make, a, of, so, than, her, and, put*	name (*Betty*), rhyming words (e.g., *Botter, butter*), two-syllable words (e.g., *batter, better*)
Golden Slumbers	5-line verses 2 sets of rhyming words	-en, -iss, -our, -ake, -en, -eep, -ot, -ill, -ing, -ock	Beginning *g, sl, k, y, sm, wh, r, pr, b, d, n, cr, w, l, th, c, h, m* Ending *n, s, ss, r, n, p, t, nd, l, ng, ck, st*	*your, you, when, baby, do, not, and, I, will, a, then, is, are, must*	new vocabulary words (*slumbers, lullaby*), plurals ending with -s (*slumbers, eyes, smiles*), rhyming words (e.g., *cry, lullaby*), multisyllable words (e.g., *golden, lullaby*)
Make New Friends	4-line poem alternate line rhyme	-ake, -ew, -end, -ut, -eep, -old	Beginning *m, n, fr, b, k, th, s, g* Ending *k, s, t, p, ld, n, r, nd*	*make, new, but, the, one, is, and*	plural adding s (*friends*), rhyming words (e.g., *old, gold*), contraction (*other's*)
Miss Mary Mack	nursery rhyme 3 sets of rhyming words	-iss, -ack, -ith, -on, -own, -een, -ent, -ant, -ump, -ey, -ome, -ill	Beginning *m, d, b, w, s, h, sh, f, c, t, th, c, j, l* Ending *s, ck, l, d, n, th, r, mp, c*	*all, in, with, down, her, back, she, mother, for, to, see, the, they, so, and, come, of*	plurals with s (*buttons, cents, elephants*), rhyming words (e.g., *Mack, back, black*), multisyllable words (e.g., *fifteen, elephants*)

WORD-ANALYSIS TEACHING OPPORTUNITIES WHEN REVISITING POETRY

Title	Type of Text (e.g., limerick, tongue twister, couplet, free verse)	Phonogram Patterns (e.g., -ack, -ome, -eep, -own)	Letter-Sound (e.g., beginning or ending consonants, consonant clusters, and consonant digraphs)	High-Frequency Words	Other (e.g., concept words; homonyms; metaphors and similes; names; new vocabulary; plurals; rhyming words; syllables)

Tools for Using Poetry

The tools for working with poetry are simple. You will want to have them well organized and readily available for quick lessons. We suggest the following:

Easel
A vertical surface for displaying chart paper, or the pocket chart, that is large enough for all children to see and sturdy enough to avoid tipping

Pocket Chart
A stiff piece of cardboard or plastic that has lines with grooves into which cards can be inserted so that children can work with lines of poems and/or individual words

Masking Cards
Cutout cardboard shapes designed to outline words on charts for children to use in locating words or parts of words

Highlighter Tape
Transparent stick-on tape that can be used to emphasize words, letters, or word parts

Sticky Notes
Small pieces of paper that have a sticky backing and can temporarily be used to conceal words or parts of words so that children can attend to them

Plain Pointers
Thin dowel rods with the tips painted red or with pencil erasers on the ends for drawing children's eyes to the print and features that you are discussing

Tags
Signs with concise directions so that children can remember an independent work activity; for example, *Read, Mix, Fix, Read* represents *Read* the poem, *Mix* up the sentence strips of a poem, *Fix* the poem back together, and *Read* it again to check it

Art Materials
Media such as paint, glue, colored paper, and tissue paper

Instructional Contexts for Poetry

Poetry fits well into the range of activities typical in second-grade classrooms.

Interactive Read-Aloud

Reading aloud forms a foundation for language and literacy development, and much poetry is meant to be read orally. In addition, reading aloud provides a model of fluent, phrased reading. There are many wonderful picture books that present rhyming verse to children in a very engaging way. For example, the *Fountas & Pinnell Classroom™ Interactive Read-Aloud Collection, Grade 2* (2018) includes rhyming books like *The Buggliest Bug* (Diggory Shields 2002), *Edward Emu* (Knowles 1988), *Edwina the Emu* (Knowles 1996), *The Pot That Juan Built* (Andrews-Goebel 2002), and *Salmon Stream* (Reed-Jones 2000).

We recommend repeated readings of favorite poems or rhyming books; it usually takes several repetitions for children to fully read it. Ask them to listen the first couple of times you read a verse, but encourage them to join in after they have grasped enough to say it with you, especially on a refrain. In this way, children will begin to internalize much of the language, enjoy it more, and also get the feeling of participating in fluent, phrased reading.

Shared Reading

Shared reading allows children to both hear the verse and see the print. You can write a poem on a chart large enough for all children to see and read in chorus. It is a great idea to put a simple illustration at the top or bottom. This gives children the idea that poetry and art go together. If you laminate this chart, you can use it again over several years. Alternatively, you can use an enlarged text like a big book from *Fountas & Pinnell Classroom™ Shared Reading Collection, Grade 2* (2018) or a chart from *Words That Sing, Grade 2: 100 Poetry Charts for Shared Reading* (2019). Such a shared approach allows you to demonstrate pointing while reading. After one or two repetitions, encourage children to read with you in interactive read-aloud. Be sure that all children can see the visual display of print. You'll want to sit or stand to the side and use a thin pointer (pointers that have objects like balls or hands on the end usually block children's view of the very word you are pointing out). You can also use translucent highlighter tape to have children show word parts, synonyms and antonyms, compound words, and spelling patterns. The idea is to maximize children's attention to the print. Shared reading helps them learn how the eyes work in reading. They'll also learn more about rhyme and rhythm.

Choral Reading and Performance

Choral reading is a more sophisticated version of shared reading. Participants may read from an enlarged text, but often they have their own individual copies. They may have a leader, but it is not always necessary for the leader to point to the words. Participants can practice reading together several times and then perform the piece. You can assign solo lines, boys' and girls' lines, question and response lines, or whole-group lines. If there is dialogue, you can assign roles. Emphasize varying the voice to suit the meaning of the poem. You can add sound effects (wooden sticks, bells, or other simple tools) or simply invite children to clap or snap their fingers to accentuate words or phrases. Children also love using hand motions.

Independent Reading

Children love reading poetry, searching for favorite poems, and illustrating poems. A personal poetry book or anthology becomes a treasure. After poems have been read in shared reading, you can reproduce them on smaller pieces of paper. Have children glue the poems into stapled or cheaply bound books with blank pages. Then invite them to decorate the covers and illustrate the poems. Be sure that you are using poems children are familiar with and can independently read. You can increase the complexity of poems for second graders. Children can also copy down, illustrate, and independently read poems from poetry books found in your classroom collections.

Writing Poetry

Children can begin to get a feel for writing verse through interactive writing. In interactive writing, you and the children compose a message together. You act as a scribe, using the easel, but occasionally children come up and write in a word or letter when you want to draw attention to it. See *Interactive Writing: How Language and Literacy Come Together, K–2* (McCarrier, Pinnell, and Fountas 2000).

You can substitute children's names in a verse or create a variation of one of their favorites (for example, for "The Months of the Year," substitute with different monthly descriptors). This activity gives them power over language and may inspire children to experiment on their own.

Types of Poetry

Poetry can be categorized in many different ways: e.g., by pattern, structure, or topic. This book includes rhymes and poems under the headings discussed below, which are related to forms, literary features, and themes. Many of the poems could be placed in more than one category.

Nursery Rhymes

Traditional rhymes by anonymous poets have been passed down over generations. There are often many different versions. Originally serving as political satire for adults, they have been loved by children for generations. They usually rhyme in couplets or alternating lines and are highly rhythmic. Young children enjoy these simple verses, and nursery rhymes help to build a foundation that will later lead them to a more sophisticated appreciation of poetry. The Mother Goose nursery rhymes, which were published in the eighteenth century, are the best known, but equivalents exist around the world. An example of a Mother Goose nursery rhyme that children love is "Old Mother Hubbard":

> Old Mother Hubbard went to the cupboard
> To give her poor dog a bone.
>
> But when she got there, the cupboard was bare,
> And so the poor dog had none.
>
> She went to the hatter's to buy him a hat.
> When she came back he was feeding the cat.
>
> She went to the barber's to buy him a wig.
> When she came back he was dancing a jig.
>
> She went to the tailor's to buy him a coat.
> When she came back he was riding a goat.
>
> She went to the cobbler's to buy him some shoes.
> When she came back he was reading the news.

Rhymed Verse

Many poems for young children have lines that end with words that rhyme. These may be *rhyming couplets* (each pair of lines rhyme), as in the poem "River":

> Runs all day and never walks,
> Often murmurs, never talks,
> It has a bed but never sleeps,
> It has a mouth but never eats.

Or, every other line may rhyme, as in Robert Louis Stevenson's poem "The Swing":

How do you like to go up in a swing,

Up in the air so blue?

Oh, I do think it the pleasantest thing

Ever a child can do!

Up in the air and over the wall,

Till I can see so wide,

Rivers and trees and cattle and all

Over the countryside—

Till I look down on the garden green,

Down on the roof so brown—

Up in the air I go flying again,

Up in the air and down!

Free Verse (Unrhymed)

Many poems evoke sensory images and sometimes have rhythm but do not
rhyme. Children will enjoy all of the different free-verse adjectives and actions, as
in those applied to sand in the poem "The Beach" found in *Sing a Song of Poetry,
Kindergarten*:

White sand,

Sea sand,

Warm sand,

Kicking sand,

Building sand,

Watching sand

As the waves roll in.

Word Play

Some poems like "The Greengrocer's Love Song" play with words by juxtaposing interesting word patterns in a humorous and playful way:

> Do you carrot all for me?
>
> My heart beets for you.
>
> With your turnip nose
>
> And your radish face
>
> You are a peach.
>
> If we cantaloupe
>
> Lettuce marry.
>
> Weed make a swell pear.

In word play, we also include *tongue twisters* (poems that are challenging to recite because they play with words that are difficult to pronounce in succession). A well-known example is the poem "How Much Wood Would a Woodchuck Chuck":

> How much wood would a woodchuck chuck
>
> If a woodchuck could chuck wood?
>
> He would chuck as much wood as a woodchuck would chuck,
>
> If a woodchuck could chuck wood.

Humorous Verse

Humorous verse draws children's attention to absurdities as well as to the sounds and rhythms of language. Sometimes these humorous verses tell nonsense stories. A good example is the poem "I Went to the Pictures Tomorrow":

> I went to the pictures tomorrow,
>
> I took a front seat at the back.
>
> I fell from the pit to the gallery,
>
> And broke a front bone in my back.
>
> A lady she gave me some chocolate,
>
> I ate it and gave it her back.
>
> I phoned for a taxi and walked it,
>
> And that's why I never came back.

Limericks

Children love limericks because of their humor, play on words, rhythm, and rhyme. They may find them easier to learn and often like to make up their own. A fun example is the poem "There was a young lad of St. Just":

> There was a young lad of St. Just
>
> Who ate apple pie till he bust;
>
> It wasn't the fru-it
>
> That caused him to do it,
>
> What finished him off was the crust.

Songs

Songs are musical texts originally intended to be sung. An example is the poem "Take Me Out to the Ball Game":

> Take me out to the ball game,
>
> Take me out with the crowd.
>
> Buy me some peanuts and Cracker Jack,
>
> I don't care if I ever get back.
>
> And it's root, root, root for the home team,
>
> If they don't win it's a shame.
>
> For it's one, two, three strikes, "You're out!"
>
> At the old ball game.

You may know the traditional tunes to the songs we have included in this volume. If you don't, compose your own or simply have children chant them while enjoying the rhythm and rhyme.

Action Songs and Poems

Action poems involve action along with rhythm and rhyme. An example is the poem "Going on a Bear Hunt":

> Would you like to go on a bear hunt?
>
> Okay—all right—come on—let's go!
>
> Open the gate—close the gate. (*clap hands*)
>
> Coming to a bridge—can't go over it—can't go under it.
>
> Let's cross it. (*march in place*)
>
> Coming to a river—can't go over it—can't go under it.
>
> Let's swim it. (*make swimming motions*)

This category also includes *jump-rope songs*, traditional rhymes that children originally chanted while they jumped rope. An example is the poem "Miss Mary Mack":

> Miss Mary Mack, Mack, Mack
>
> All dressed in black, black, black
>
> With silver buttons, buttons, buttons
>
> All down her back, back, back.
>
> She asked her mother, mother, mother
>
> For fifteen cents, cents, cents
>
> To see the elephants, elephants, elephants
>
> Jump the fence, fence, fence.
>
> They jumped so high, high, high
>
> They touched the sky, sky, sky,
>
> And they didn't come down, down, down
>
> Till the fourth of July, ly, ly.

Children can chant and act out jump-rope songs. There are also chants that accompany games or are simply enjoyable to say together. Chants, like songs, showcase rhythm and rhyme; they are meant to be spoken in chorus rather than set to music. For example, "A Sailor Went to Sea" is rhythmical with a fast pace and alliteration:

> A sailor went to sea, sea, sea
>
> To see what he could see, see, see
>
> But all that he could see, see, see
>
> Was the bottom of the deep blue sea, sea, sea.

Concept Poems

Poems in this category focus on concepts such as numbers, days of the week, colors, ordinal words, seasons, time of day or night, and any other category of information. An example is the poem "Bunnies' Bedtime":

> "My bunnies must go to bed,"
>
> The little mother rabbit said.
>
> "But I will count them first to see
>
> If they have all come back to me.
>
> One bunny, two bunnies, three bunnies dear,
>
> Four bunnies, five bunnies—yes, all are here.
>
> They are the prettiest things alive—
>
> My bunnies, one, two, three, four, five."

These verses are not only engaging but also easy to learn. As children learn them, they will be repeating the vocabulary that surrounds important concepts.

In the category of concept poems, we also include name poems, which really transcend categories. Many verses present a wonderful opportunity to substitute children's names for names or words already there. In the poem "Susie Moriar," substitute different children's names for *Susie*. Other poems, like "Bullfrog," have blank lines for children to fill in their names.

Many of the poems in the book also offer similar innovations, so look for opportunities. Children will love substituting their own words and phrases. They will develop ownership for the writing and, in the process, become more sensitive to rhymes, syllables, and word patterns.

Fifty Ways to Use Poems—Plus!

Below we suggest fifty specific ways to use the poems in this volume. Plus, you will notice that each poem includes an instructional suggestion: an easy way to refine and extend the learning and enjoyment potential of each poem. You will find many more ways to engage children in joyful play with oral and written language. The rich collection of poems in this volume can be reproduced, analyzed, or simply read aloud. Enjoy!

Decisions about using poetry depend on your purposes for instruction and the age of the children. By going over favorites again and again, children will internalize rhymes and develop awareness of new language structures. They will become more sensitive to the sounds of language and take pleasure in it. Try out the following suggestions as appropriate to second grade:

1. **Marching to rhymes** Marching around the room while chanting a poem will help children feel the rhythm.

2. **Puppet show** Have children make stick, finger, or sock puppets of their favorite characters in poems and act out the poem as their friends read it. Alternatively, have the puppet say the poem.

3. **Storyboards** Have children draw or paint a backdrop that represents the scene from a rhyme or song. Then have them make cutout figures and glue them on popsicle sticks so that they can move the puppets around in front of the backdrop.

4. **Listening for rhymes** Have children clap or snap their fingers when they come to a rhyming word. They can also say the rhyming word softer (or louder) or mouth the word without making a sound.

5. **Responding** Divide the class in half. Taking a familiar poem, have half the group read (or say) the poem up to the rhyming word and then stop. Let the other half of the class shout the rhyming word.

6. **Recorded poems** Record specific poems on a device so that children can listen independently at a listening center. Include card stock copies of the poems, and show children how to follow along with the recordings.

7. **Class poetry recording** As children learn poems, gradually add to a class recording of their poetry reading or chanting. Keep a table of contents for the audio on a chart and/or place the taped poems in a book. Children can listen to the audio while following along in the book.

8. **Poem pictures** After reading a poem aloud at different times of the day, have children make pictures to go with it and display them with the poem. Duplicate individual copies of a simple poem, and ask each child to illustrate it.

9. **Base Words and Affixes** Write the poem in large print on a chart or on strips for a pocket chart. After many readings of a poem on a large chart, help children notice prefixes or suffixes. They can use a masking card or highlighter tape to mark affixes.

10. **Poem innovations** Engage children in noticing and using the language syntax in the poem to create their own similar versions. For example, insert different names in the poem "Fooba Wooba, John" or different foods in the poem "If All the Little Raindrops."

11. **Personal poetry books** Have children make their own personal poetry books by gluing the poems they experienced in shared reading into spiral notebooks and then illustrating them. Over time they will have a large personal collection of poems to take home.

12. **Little poem books** Make individual poem books, with one or two lines of a poem on each page (for example, "I Never Saw a Purple Cow" by Gelett Burgess). Children can illustrate each page, read the book, and take it home.

13. **Poem performances** Children can perform the poems after they learn them by sometimes adding sound effects with rhythm instruments such as sticks and drums or by clapping and snapping their fingers.

14. **Responsive reading** Find poems such as "Knock, Knock" or "Five Waiting Pumpkins" that lend themselves to recitation by two or more speakers. Groups of children read questions and answers or alternate lines.

15. **Poetry play** Lead children in saying their favorite poems while they line up, as they walk through an area in which their talking will not disturb other classes, or any time they have a moment of wait time.

16. **Line-up poems** When passing out of the room for recess or lunch, play games in which children say or finish a line of a poem in order to take their place in line.

17. **Rhyming or repeating cloze** Read poems, asking children to join in only on the rhyming words. Put highlighter tape on the rhyming or repeated words.

18. **Finger poems and action poems** Make finger plays from poems. Act out poems with motions involving the entire body. We have included finger play and action directions for many poems, but you can make up many more.

19. **Poem posters** Use art materials (colored and/or textured paper, pens, crayons, paints) to illustrate poems on charts for the whole group to enjoy or for children to enjoy individually in their personal poetry books.

20. **Poems with blanks** Give children individual copies of poems with a blank space in which they can write their names.

21. **Mystery words** In shared reading of a familiar poem, leave out key words but show the first letter so that children can check their reading. You can also use sticky notes and then uncover the word to check it.

22. **Synonym and antonym hunt** Keep an ongoing chart of synonyms and antonyms that children notice in poems.

23. **Poetry box** Make a poetry box that contains slightly enlarged and illustrated versions of familiar poems; children can take them out and read them to a classmate.

24. **Poetry board** Make a theme poetry board using poems that explore a concept (for example, animals or food).

25. **Tongue twisters** Make up tongue twisters using the names of children in the class and have them illustrate the verses: for example, *Carlos carries cookies, carrots, candy, and cucumbers in a cart.*

26. **Pocket chart** Place poems on sentence strips in a pocket chart for a variety of activities: substituting words to innovate on the text; highlighting words, letters, or parts of words with colored highlighter tape; putting sentence strips in order for reading; and masking words to make predictions.

27. **Poem puzzles** Have children cut a poem into strips, mix them up, order them, and glue them on paper in the correct order. Then have them use art materials to illustrate the text. Create a simple strip template to photocopy for many different poems.

28. **Ways to compare** Keep an ongoing chart of comparisons that children find in poems. Encourage children to "borrow" similes and metaphors for their own writing.

29. **Sequencing poems** Once they have internalized a poem, kindergarteners can write one line of a simple poem on separate pages, staple the pages together as a book, illustrate the pages, and then read their books to others.

30. **More songs and poems** Be on the alert for popular songs that children like or street rhymes that they know. Take appropriate verses from these songs and add them to the poetry collection.

31. **Poem plays** Create a play from the poem. Read the poem (children may join in) while several children act it out.

32. **Sound words** Keep an ongoing list of onomatopoetic words that children find in poems.

33. **Poetry party** Have a party to which everyone comes dressed as a character from a poem (props may be made of paper). The group has to guess which poem is represented and then read the poem to the child representing that character.

34. **Character bulletin board** Each child draws a favorite character from a poem and then cuts the figure out. Use interactive writing to create labels for each character on the board.

35. **Poem mashup** Take two favorite poetry characters and have them "meet" each others' poems by including or switching their names.

36. **Favorite poetry recording** Prepare a poetry recording of the children's favorite poems, paper copies of which you can place in a box. Ask the principal, librarian, parents, and other teachers to contribute to the recordings. Children will enjoy listening to the different voices and following the words.

37. **Poetry picnic** Many poems have something to do with food: for example, "The Donut Song." After children have learned a lot of verses, make a list of foods. Consider bringing in samples of the food your class listed. Then children can read or say the poem while eating the food. Be sure to check with families for food allergies and to get permission.

38. **Poetry pairs** Children find two poems that go together in some way. They bring the two poems to sharing time and tell how they are alike. You can make a class book of poem pairs with (illustrated) connected poems on opposite pages.

39. **Poetry landscape mural** Children paint a background landscape on which they can glue different poetry characters. This mural requires some planning. For example, you would need to draw the crooked mile and maybe the crooked house in the poem "There Was a Crooked Man."

40. **Poetry sort** Have a box of poems on cards that children know very well and can read. They can read the poems and sort them in any way they want to: e.g., theme (happy, silly, sad), topic (mice, girls, boys, bears), and the way they rhyme (two lines, every other line, partial rhyme, no rhyme).

41. **Poems in shapes** Have children read a poem and then glue the poem on a shape (give them a template) that represents it. For example, the poem "Snow" could be placed on or near a window during wintertime.

42. **Mixed-up poem** Place a familiar poem on sentence strips in the pocket chart. Mix it up and have children help you rebuild it by saying the lines and looking for the next one. You can also have a correct model displayed beside the cut-up version so that they can check it. Soon children will be able to perform this action on their own.

43. **Picture words** Have children draw pictures for key words in a poem and display them right above the word on a chart.

44. **Hunting for words** Using flyswatters with rectangular holes in the center (or masking cards), have children hunt for particular words, words that rhyme, or words that start like another.

45. **Word location** Display a familiar poem in the pocket chart, but leave some blanks. Give children the missing key words. Stop when you come to the key word, and ask who has it. Children will need to think about beginning sounds and letters when finding where they go.

46. **Homophone and homograph list** Look for words that can be connected (homonyms), and talk about how they are used in funny ways.

47. **Builder poem** Give each child in a group one word from a poem, written in large print on a card. Have the rest of the class line up these children so that the word order is correct. Then have children take turns walking down the line and saying the poem by pointing to each child and his or her word. Alternatively, have children place the cards in a pocket chart one at a time. They will have to notice when their assigned words come next.

48. **Looking at high-frequency words** The words children encounter over and over in poems will form a core of words that they know and can quickly recognize. When looking for new words, be sure to include ones with more complex spellings. Encourage children to select words from poems to place on their "Words to Learn" lists. You can have them locate the words to draw attention to them. An interesting exercise is to create high-frequency words in different fonts. Be sure the words are clear and recognizable. Matching these words to words on a chart or in the pocket chart creates an additional challenge in looking at letter features.

49. **Poetry newsletter** Send home a monthly newsletter that tells parents the poems children have learned and provides some poems they can sing or say at home.

50. **Great words** As the class reads poetry together, keep an ongoing list of words children love. Choose powerful verbs and adjectives. Children can use this list to help make their writing more interesting.

Poetry Links to Phonics Lessons

In *Fountas & Pinnell Phonics, Spelling, and Word Study Lessons, Grade 2* (2019) under Connect Learning Across Contexts, you will find Shared Reading recommendations that enable you to connect learning across the contexts shown in A Design for Responsive Literacy Teaching. Often, the recommendations suggest you turn to *Sing a Song of Poetry* for instructional follow-up using particular poems, songs, and verse. This list links many phonics lessons to a specific poem that extends and refines the instructional aim of the lesson; however, you will notice that not all lessons are linked to a poem, and sometimes, a lesson is linked to two or more poems. What does this mean? The links are completely flexible! Feel free to find and make your own links, and do not feel compelled to use every poem we recommend.

The primary goal of this collection is, quite literally, to sing a song of poetry! Invite children to chant, recite, echo, and play with the poems. Above all, *Sing a Song of Poetry* is meant to inspire a love of language.

Letter-Sound Relationships

LSR 1 Afternoon on a Hill; My Father Is Extremely Tall; Miss Polly Had a Dolly

LSR 2 The Donut Song; Found a Peanut; I'm a Frozen Icicle

LSR 3 Stepping Stones; Sneeze on Monday; Spread It Thick

LSR 4 December Leaves; Mr. Crocodile; Spring Is Coming

LSR 5 Stepping Stones; The Boy Stood in the Supper-Room; Clouds

LSR 6 The Goat; Away Down East; Rain

LSR 7 I Like Silver; Five Waiting Pumpkins; Sing Your Way Home

LSR 8 Bed in Summer; Calico Pie; Rain

LSR 9 Fuzzy Little Caterpillar; Golden Slumbers; The City Mouse and the Garden Mouse

LSR 10 How Much Wood Would a Woodchuck Chuck; The Codfish; The North Wind Doth Blow

LSR 11	Walking Through the Jungle; Eletelephony; Wash the Dishes
LSR 12	Little Arabella Miller; Bunnies' Bedtime; Terrific Toes
LSR 13	Found a Peanut; Away Down East; Elephant
LSR 14	The Littlest Worm; The House That Jack Built; Walk Fast
LSR 15	Elephant; The Animal Fair; The Land of Counterpane
LSR 16	How Much Wood Would a Woodchuck Chuck; The City Mouse and the Garden Mouse; Teacher, Teacher
LSR 17	Over the River and Through the Wood; The Goat; I Live in the City
LSR 18	Down by the Bay; Fiddle-i-fee; The Goat
LSR 19	Found a Peanut; The Greedy Man; I Raised a Great Hullabaloo
LSR 20	Five Little Owls; The City Mouse and the Garden Mouse; The Boy Stood in the Supper-Room
LSR 21	The Moon; I Raised a Great Hullabaloo; The Brook
LSR 22	Afternoon on a Hill; Calico Pie; Down by the Bay
LSR 23	Pairs or Pears; The Animal Fair; The Bear

Spelling Patterns

SP 1	If All the Little Raindrops; One Bottle of Pop; There's a Hole in the Bucket
SP 2	Higgledy, Piggledy, See How They Run; Milkman, Milkman; One Bottle of Pop
SP 3	Good Morning, Merry Sunshine!; Old King Cole; Sing Your Way Home
SP 4	Take Me Out to the Ball Game; Make New Friends; The Greedy Man
SP 5	Good Morning, Merry Sunshine!; At the Seaside; Queen, Queen Caroline
SP 6	Stepping Stones; Old King Cole; Sing Your Way Home
SP 7	Afternoon on a Hill; She Sells Seashells; Miss Mary Mack
SP 8	Nest Eggs; Good, Better, Best; Walk Fast
SP 9	The Swing; Spring Is Coming; In the Morning
SP 10	Elephant; Spread It Thick; The Animal Fair
SP 11	Clouds; There Was a Young Farmer of Leeds; The Land of Counterpane
SP 12	How Much Wood Would a Woodchuck Chuck; Good Morning, Merry Sunshine!; The Moon
SP 13	Rain; If All the Little Raindrops; I've Been Working on the Railroad
SP 14	The Goat; Five Cream Buns; If All the Little Raindrops
SP 15	Down by the Bay; The Fox Went Out on a Chilly Night; Five Cream Buns
SP 16	The City Mouse and the Garden Mouse; There Was a Young Farmer of Leeds; The Swing
SP 17	Bed in Summer; Buttercups and Daisies; Caterpillar

High-Frequency Words

Word Meaning/Vocabulary

Word Structure

WS 15 Mr. Nobody; Monday's Child; The Months of the Year

WS 16 If Wishes Were Horses; Wash the Dishes

WS 17 Birds of a Feather; Five Fat Turkeys; The Land of Counterpane

WS 18 Buttercups and Daisies; Bunnies' Bedtime; The Months of the Year

WS 19 December Leaves; The Months of the Year; The Moon

WS 20 Good Morning, Merry Sunshine; Buffalo Gals; Two Little Kittens

WS 21 Little Arabella Miller; The Codfish; The House That Jack Built

WS 22 Taking Off; A Fairy Went A-marketing; The Bear

WS 23 My Shadow; Skip to My Lou; Afternoon on a Hill

WS 24 Teacher, Teacher; The Tutor; The Bus

WS 25 Old King Cole; Teacher, Teacher; Calico Pie

WS 26 The Donut Song; Cradle Song; I'm a Frozen Icicle

WS 27 Bed in Summer; I Hear Thunder; Once I Saw a Bunny

WS 28 A Twister of Twists; A Nonsense Alphabet

Word-Solving Actions

WSA 1 Bed in Summer; I Live in the City; The Orchestra

WSA 2 The Secret; The Goat; Miss Mary Mack

WSA 3 A Thunderstorm; The Orchestra; Over in the Meadow

WSA 4 Down by the Bay; Clouds; Old Mother Hubbard

WSA 5 Caterpillar; The Chickens; Combinations

WSA 6 Fuzzy Little Caterpillar; Eletelephony; Fooba Wooba, John

WSA 7 The Moon; Cradle Song; Old Mother Hubbard

WSA 8 Caterpillar; *A*, My Name Is Alice; Buttercups and Daisies

WSA 9 Out and In; John Jacob Jingleheimer Schmidt; Take Me Out to the Ball Game

WSA 10 New Sights; Gregory Griggs; My Old Hen

WSA 11 The Moon; Spring Is Coming; Away Down East

WSA 12 The City Mouse and the Garden Mouse, There Was a Little Girl

WSA 13 I Went to the Pictures Tomorrow; Walking Through the Jungle; I Thought

WSA 14 December Leaves; In the Morning; Pairs or Pears

WSA 15 Betty Botter; *A*, My Name Is Alice; The Hobbyhorse

WSA 16 The Centipede's Song; I Hear Thunder; The Secret

2 Y's

2 Y's U R.

2 Y's U B.

I C U R

2 Y's 4 me!

© 2019 by Irene C. Fountas and Gay Su Pinnell from *Sing a Song of Poetry, Grade 2*. Portsmouth, NH: Heinemann. May be photocopied for classroom use only.

fold here

SUGGESTION: Understanding this poem will require reading it aloud. In partners, have children read the poem to each other. Then invite the whole group to talk about how names of numbers and letters create the poem's meaning. End by reading the poem together as a class and then asking children to write their own messages using numbers and letters.

A, My Name Is Alice

A, my name is Alice,
And my husband's name is Al.
We come from Alabama,
And we sell apples.

B, my name is Barbara,
And my husband's name is Bob.
We come from Boston,
And we sell beans.

C, my name is Carol,
And my husband's name is Carl.
We come from Chicago,
And we sell carts.

D, my name is Donna,
And my husband's name is Dave.
We come from Denver,
And we sell doughnuts.

E, my name is Ellen,
And my husband's name is Ed.
We come from Evanston,
And we sell eggs.

F, my name is Frances,
And my husband's name is Frank.
We come from Florida,
And we sell frankfurters.

SUGGESTION: After the class is familiar with this alphabet-game poem, invite them to create an illustrated class book that highlights each classmate's first name. Ask children to play with the poem as they write personalized stanzas. For example, instead of writing *my husband's name is*, children can write *my pet's name is, my sister's name is, my imaginary friend's name is*, etc. It can be anyone's name, so long as the name starts with the first letter of the child's name. After children write their stanzas, have them illustrate their work before adding it to the class book.

Afternoon on a Hill

by Edna St. Vincent Millay

I will be the gladdest thing

Under the sun.

I will touch a hundred flowers

And not pick one.

I will look at cliffs and clouds

With quiet eyes,

Watch the wind bow down the grass,

And the grass rise.

And when lights begin to show

Up from the town,

I will mark which must be mine,

And then start down!

SUGGESTION: Millay's beautiful poem invites children to think about the simplicity of nature. Use it to stimulate a discussion about how to care for and value the earth. While reciting the poem, have children act out the lines: e.g., being the grass that bows over in the wind but rises back up. Pair it with the picture book *Our Big Home: An Earth Poem* by Linda Glaser (2000) found in the *Fountas & Pinnell Classroom™ Interactive Read-Aloud Collection, Grade 2* (2018) or the picture book *Miss Rumphius* by Barbara Cooney (1982).

fold here

Aiken Drum

There was a man lived in the moon,
Lived in the moon, lived in the moon.
There was a man lived in the moon,
And his name was Aiken Drum.

Chorus

> *And he played upon a ladle,*
> *A ladle, a ladle,*
> *He played upon a ladle,*
> *And his name was Aiken Drum.*

And his hat was made of good cream cheese,
Of good cream cheese, of good cream cheese,
And his hat was made of good cream cheese,
And his name was Aiken Drum.

Repeat Chorus

ADDITIONAL VERSES:

And his coat was made of good roast beef,
Of good roast beef, of good roast beef,
And his coat was made of good roast beef,
And his name was Aiken Drum.

Repeat Chorus

And his pants were made of plastic bags,
Of plastic bags, of plastic bags,
And his pants were made of plastic bags,
And his name was Aiken Drum.

Repeat Chorus

fold here

SUGGESTION: This rhyme lends itself to creating more verses. After children have learned the poem and have a feeling for the rhythm and pattern of repetition and rhyme, ask them to work in partners or trios to create a verse using a theme. Then have children take turns performing their creations.

Animal Crackers

by Christopher Morley

Animal crackers and cocoa to drink,
That is the finest of suppers, I think;
When I'm grown up and can have what I please,
I think I shall always insist upon these.

What do you choose when you're offered a treat?
When Mother says, "What would you like best to eat?"
Is it waffles and syrup, or cinnamon toast?
It's cocoa and animals that I love the most!

The kitchen's the cosiest place that I know;
The kettle is singing, the stove is aglow,
And there in the twilight, how jolly to see
The cocoa and animals waiting for me.

Daddy and Mother dine later in state,
With Mary to cook for them, Susan to wait;
But they don't have nearly as much fun as I
Who eat in the kitchen with Nurse standing by;
And Daddy once said he would like to be me
Having cocoa and animals once more for tea!

© 2019 by Irene C. Fountas and Gay Su Pinnell from *Sing a Song of Poetry, Grade 2*. Portsmouth, NH: Heinemann. May be photocopied for classroom use only.

SUGGESTION: Read this poem aloud together as a class. You may need to define its archaic language and concepts: e.g., *aglow* and *Nurse*. Afterwards, invite children to talk about their favorite food and drink. On chart paper, record their replies. Then divide the class into four groups—one for each stanza. Have children in each group substitute *animal crackers* and cocoa for a new food and drink combination—the sillier the better! Then ask each group to recite its revised stanza on cue.

fold here

The Animal Fair

I went to the animal fair

The birds and the beasts were there.

The big baboon by the light of the moon

Was combing his auburn hair.

The monkey bumped the skunk,

And sat on the elephant's trunk;

The elephant sneezed and fell to his knees,

And that was the end of the monk,

The monk, the monk, the monk,

The monk, the monk, the monk.

© 2019 by Irene C. Fountas and Gay Su Pinnell from *Sing a Song of Poetry, Grade 2.* Portsmouth, NH: Heinemann. May be photocopied for classroom use only.

SUGGESTION: Children will enjoy the funny images in this traditional rhyme. Move along at a good pace and have them think of different ways to perform it: e.g., clap hands to keep the beat or say the last two lines in a dwindling whisper. Alternatively, have some children softly and rhythmically chant *the monk* throughout the song while others sing or chant the lines, joining in unison on the last two.

Answer to a Child's Question

by Samuel Taylor Coleridge

Do you ask what the birds say? The sparrow, the dove,

The linnet and thrush say, "I love and I love!"

In the winter they're silent—the wind is so strong;

What it says, I don't know, but it sings a loud song.

But green leaves, and blossoms, and sunny warm weather,

And singing, and loving—all come back together.

But the lark is so brimful of gladness and love,

The green fields below him, the blue sky above,

That he sings, and he sings; and for ever sings he—

"I love my Love, and my Love loves me!"

SUGGESTION: Children may need you to explain what a *sparrow*, a *dove*, a *linnet*, and a *thrush* are (different kinds of birds). Play a recording for children of each bird's unique song. Then invite the class to recite the whole poem. When children recite what the birds say ("*I love and I love!*" and "*I love my Love, and my Love loves me!*"), play back a recording of one of the bird's calls. Alternatively, on low, play one or more of the bird calls while the class recites the poem.

fold here

Apples Are Red

Apples are red,

My nose is blue,

Standing at the bus stop,

Waiting for you.

SUGGESTION: This poem is a variation of "Roses Are Red." Once the class is familiar with the poem's rhythm and pattern, assign partners or divide children into small groups. Then invite them to create new variations using different food or drink, different colors, different parts of the body, and different actions: e.g., *Bananas are yellow. / My eyes are brown. / Hanging from the treetops, / I dropped my crown.*

As I Was Going to Banbury

As I was going to Banbury,

All on a summer's day,

My wife had butter, eggs, and cheese,

And I had corn and hay.

Bob drove the cows and Tom the swine,

Dick led the foal and mare.

I sold them all, then home again,

We came from Banbury fair.

SUGGESTION: Use this poem as an opportunity to focus on rhythm. Invite children to recite it together while tapping or clapping to the rhythm as a way to reinforce the poem's cadence. This poem is also a good example of how some rhyming words end with letters that match while others do not: e.g., *day* and *hay* versus *mare* and *fair*.

fold here

At the Seaside

by Robert Louis Stevenson

When I was down beside the sea,

A wooden spade they gave to me

To dig the sandy shore.

My holes were empty like a cup.

In every hole the sea came up

Till it could come no more.

fold here

SUGGESTION: Spend some time talking about the meaning of the poem and mentally picturing the empty holes gradually filling up with seawater. Some children may not understand the concept that the water is under the sand and seeps in.

At the Zoo

by William Makepeace Thackeray

First I saw the white bear, then I saw the black;

Then I saw the camel with a hump upon his back;

Then I saw the gray wolf, with mutton in his maw;

Then I saw the wombat waddle in the straw;

Then I saw the elephant a-waving of his trunk;

Then I saw the monkeys—mercy, how unpleasantly they smelt!

fold here

SUGGESTION: Children will enjoy the rhythm ad cadence of this verse. Have them chant each line with increasing emphasis and volume. Model how to stop in the middle of the final line—at *mercy*—to add vocal flair and humor. You may want to show a picture of a wombat. Once they see a picture, they will understand why *waddle* might be an appropriate word. Be sure to also define unfamiliar words like *mutton* and *maw*.

Away Down East

Away down east, away down west,

Away down Alabama,

The only girl that I like best,

Her name is Susie Anna.

I took her to a ball one night

And sat her down to supper.

The table fell and she fell, too

And stuck her nose in the butter.

The butter, the butter,

The yellow margarine.

Two black eyes, and a jelly nose

And all the rest turned green.

fold here

SUGGESTION: Divide the children into three groups and have each group read a verse. This is a good poem to use when trying to locate two-, three-, and four-syllable words all on one page.

The Bear

The other day   (The other day)
I met a bear,   (I met a bear,)
Away up there,   (Away up there,)
A great big bear!   (A great big bear!)

The other day I met a bear, away up there, a great big bear!

He looked at me,   (He looked at me,)
I looked at him.   (I looked at him.)
He sized up me,   (He sized up me,)
I sized up him.   (I sized up him.)

He looked at me, I looked at him. He sized up me, I sized up him.

And so I ran   (And so I ran)
Away from there.   (Away from there.)
And right behind   (And right behind)
Me was that bear.   (Me was that bear.)

And so I ran away from there. And right behind me was that bear.

Ahead of me   (Ahead of me)
I saw a tree,   (I saw a tree,)
A great big tree,   (A great big tree,)
Oh, golly gee!   (Oh, golly gee!)

Ahead of me I saw a tree, a great big tree, oh, golly gee!

continued

The lowest branch	(The lowest branch)
Was ten feet up.	(Was ten feet up.)
I had to jump	(I had to jump)
And trust my luck.	(And trust my luck.)

The lowest branch was ten feet up. I had to jump and trust my luck.

And so I jumped	(And so I jumped)
Into the air,	(Into the air,)
And missed that branch	(And missed that branch)
Away up there.	(Away up there.)

And so I jumped into the air, and missed that branch away up there.

Now don't you fret,	(Now don't you fret,)
And don't you frown.	(And don't you frown.)
I caught that branch	(I caught that branch)
On the way back down.	(On the way back down.)

Now don't you fret, and don't you frown. I caught that branch on the way back down.

That's all there is,	(That's all there is,)
There is no more,	(There is no more,)
Until I meet	(Until I meet)
That bear once more.	(That bear once more.)

That's all there is, there is no more, until I meet that bear once more.

© 2019 by Irene C. Fountas and Gay Su Pinnell from *Sing a Song of Poetry, Grade 2.* Portsmouth, NH: Heinemann. May be photocopied for classroom use only.

fold here

SUGGESTION: This poem uses an echo technique; words and phrases repeat throughout this story about a meeting with a bear. This is a good poem for English language learners. Children can listen to and repeat one line at a time. And then everyone in unison repeats each four-line stanza as one line.

Bed in Summer

by Robert Louis Stevenson

In winter I get up at night
And dress by yellow candlelight.
In summer, quite the other way,
I have to go to bed by day.

I have to go to bed and see
The birds still hopping on the tree,
Or hear the grown-up people's feet
Still going past me in the street.

And does it not seem hard to you,
When all the sky is clear and blue,
And I should like so much to play,
To have to go to bed by day?

SUGGESTION: Invite the class to read this poem aloud multiple times. Then return to each stanza and ask children to talk about what the poet meant. Many children will agree with the last stanza: it's hard to go to bed when the sun is still out. Have them talk about what seasons have longer days, what seasons have shorter days, and what time of the year this poem probably takes place in. Pair this poem with the picture book *On Earth* by G. Brian Karas (2005) found in the *Fountas & Pinnell Classroom™ Interactive Read-Aloud Collection, Grade 2* (2018).

fold here

Bees

A swarm of bees in May,

Is worth a load of hay.

A swarm of bees in June,

Is worth a silver spoon.

A swarm of bees in July,

Isn't worth a fly.

fold here

SUGGESTION: After children are familiar with the words, invite them to divide into three groups, each reciting two lines apiece. This proverbial bee-keeper's saying suggests that the later it is in the year, the less time for bees to collect pollen from blossoming flowers. Encourage children to talk about why a swarm of bees' worth varies during different months of the season or year. Pair this poem with the nonfiction book *The Honey Makers* by Gail Gibbons (1997) found in the *Fountas & Pinnell Classroom™ Interactive Read-Aloud Collection, Grade 2* (2018) or the nonfiction book *From Flower to Honey* by June Schwartz found in the *Fountas & Pinnell Classroom™ Shared Reading Collection, Grade 2* (2018).

Betty Botter

Betty Botter bought some butter,

"But," she said, "this butter's bitter;

If I put it in my batter,

It will make my batter bitter.

But a bit of better butter

Will make my batter better."

So she bought a bit of butter

Better than her bitter butter,

And she put it in her batter.

So 'twas better Betty Botter

Bought a bit of better butter.

© 2019 by Irene C. Fountas and Gay Su Pinnell from *Sing a Song of Poetry, Grade 2*. Portsmouth, NH: Heinemann. May be photocopied for classroom use only.

SUGGESTION: Some students, especially English language learners, may need help with words like *batter* and *bitter*. Children love to say this verse slowly the first time, and then increase their speed on subsequent readings—all while trying not to mispronounce the words! Use this poem as children learn to identify short vowel sounds, and revisit it again when focusing on double consonants in the middle of words.

fold here

Big Ship Sailing

There's a big ship sailing on the illy ally oh,

Illy ally oh, illy ally oh.

There's a big ship sailing on the illy ally oh,

Hi, ho, illy ally oh.

There's a big ship sailing, rocking on the sea,

Rocking on the sea, rocking on the sea.

There's a big ship sailing, rocking on the sea,

Hi, ho, rocking on the sea.

There's a big ship sailing back again,

Back again, back again.

There's a big ship sailing back again,

Hi, ho, back again.

SUGGESTION: Children love to sing this song as they follow an appointed captain around the room. Invite children to pretend to be the ship or the ship's passengers who *toot* and *salute* as the ship leaves the dock. Help children make up additional verses featuring other kinds of boats and ships with the appropriate descriptive words: e.g., *tugboats chugging, sailboats tacking,* and *fireboats standing by.* Accompany this song with its recording from John Langstaff's CD *Songs for Singing Children.*

Birds of a Feather

Birds of a feather flock together

And so do pigs and swine.

Rats and mice will have their choice,

And so will I have mine.

SUGGESTION: This seemingly simple verse has a deeper meaning. Read the poem to the class and ask children to listen closely to the words. Then invite them to join in reading the poem together. Afterwards, help children to reflect on and articulate what the words might mean under the surface.

fold here

The Boy Stood in the Supper-room

The boy stood in the supper-room

Whence all but he had fled;

He'd eaten seven pots of jam

And he was gorged with bread.

"Oh, one more crust before I bust!"

He cried in accents wild;

He licked the plates, he sucked the spoons—

He was a vulgar child.

There came a burst of thunder-sound—

The boy—Oh! Where was he?

Asked of the maid who mopped him up,

The bread crumbs and the tea!

SUGGESTION: Children will probably need to hear this poem a few times before it makes sense. Though they may infer the definition of unfamiliar words like *supper-room* and *gorged*, you may need to define archaic language like *Whence* and *vulgar*. Teach children that this is a "cautionary tale." What does it warn them about? Pairing this poem with Maurice Sendak's book *Pierre: A Cautionary Tale in Five Acts and a Prologue* will give children another experience with the genre.

Bring the Wagon Home, John

Oh, bring the wagon home, John.

It will not hold us all.

We used to ride around in it,

When you and I were small.

fold here

SUGGESTION: This poem may inspire children to reminisce about toys or belongings they keep even though they are too old for them. Invite them to discuss why the speaker wants to keep the wagon even though she (or he) and John have outgrown it. Then ask children to rewrite the poem using a favorite toy or belonging they have since outgrown, but still keep. Afterwards, have them illustrate their personalized adaptations.

The Brook

Grumbling, stumbling,

Fumbling all the day;

Fluttering, stuttering,

Muttering away;

Rustling, hustling,

Rustling as it flows;

This is how the brook talks,

Bubbling as it goes.

SUGGESTION: Read the poem aloud as a class until its words and rhythm are familiar. Then ask children to talk about why the poet chose these particular words to describe the brook's motion. You may need to clarify what a *brook* is before children can think about its movement. Afterwards, invite them to discuss how a nonliving thing, such as a brook, can *talk*. What other nonliving things can be described like a living thing in this way? For example, ideas may include how the wind whispers or howls.

Buffalo Gals

As I was walking down the street,
Down the street, down the street,
A pretty little gal I chanced to meet,
Oh, she was fair to see.

Chorus

> *Buffalo Gals, won't you come out tonight,*
> *Come out tonight, come out tonight?*
> *Buffalo Gals, won't you come out tonight,*
> *And dance by the light of the moon?*

I stopped her and we had a talk,
Had a talk, had a talk,
Her feet took up the whole sidewalk,
And left no room for me.

Repeat Chorus

I asked her if she'd have a dance,
Have a dance, have a dance,
I thought that I might have a chance,
To shake a foot with her.

Repeat Chorus

I danced with a gal with a hole in her stocking,
And her heel kept a-knocking, and her toes kept a-rocking.
I danced with a gal with a hole in her stocking,
And we danced by the light of the moon.

Repeat Chorus

SUGGESTION: Read this rhythmic song aloud to children in the class. Then ask them to notice the rhyming pattern of the verses and choruses. Afterwards, invite children to sing the poem together while one child shakes a tambourine during the chorus to help keep the beat.

fold here

Bullfrog

Here's Mr. Bullfrog,

Sitting on a rock.

Along comes _____.

Mr. Bullfrog jumps, KERPLOP!

fold here

SUGGESTION: Children enjoy reciting this verse because they get to insert names of classmates and jump off imaginary rocks as they shout *KERPLOP!* Revisit this poem when you begin discussing abbreviations. Try adding *Mr.* or *Ms.* and the child's surname as a way to compliment *Mr. Bullfrog*.

Bunnies' Bedtime

"My bunnies must go to bed,"

The little mother rabbit said.

"But I will count them first to see

If they have all come back to me.

One bunny, two bunnies, three bunnies dear,

Four bunnies, five bunnies—yes, all are here.

They are the prettiest things alive—

My bunnies, one, two, three, four, five."

SUGGESTION: Assign one child to be the mother bunny and five other children to be her baby bunnies. Invite the rest of the class to recite the poem while their classmates act out their roles: e.g., mother bunny looks around for her baby bunnies and one by one, on cue, each baby bunny pops out of his or her hiding spot. After the class performs the poem, invite children to substitute different animals before switching roles so all have a turn to act.

fold here

The Bus

There is a painted bus,

With twenty painted seats,

It carries painted people

Along the painted streets.

They pull the painted bell,

The painted driver stops,

And they all get out together

At the little painted shops.

SUGGESTION: After reading the poem aloud, have children talk about what the poet is describing. Ask them what word is repeated over and over (*painted*) to help them figure out what the poem describes (a painted scene). Invite children to paint the scene from the poem, either individually or as a whole class. Make sure they add every detail from the poem. Then ask for volunteers to share their artwork.

Buttercups and Daisies

Buttercups and daisies,

Oh what pretty flowers,

Coming in the springtime,

To tell of sunny hours!

While the trees are leafless,

While the fields are bare,

Buttercups and daisies,

Spring up everywhere.

SUGGESTION: Ask children to share with you what they know about flowers. How many kinds can they think of? Make a class list together. Then illustrate the list with the help of picture books like Anita Lobel's *Allison's Zinnia*, an ABC book with paintings of twenty-six different flowers.

fold here

The Butterfly

April

Come she will,

May

She will stay,

June

She'll change her tune,

July

She will fly,

August

Die she must.

SUGGESTION: Point out the unique structure of this poem with one-word lines followed with a rhyming description. This poem indirectly suggests the life cycle of a butterfly from April to August. Children can talk about what each stage means (including *change her tune*, which means turning from a pupa to a butterfly). They may want to consult some informational books and produce drawings of each stage to illustrate the poem.

Calico Pie

by Edward Lear

I
Calico pie,
The little birds fly
Down to the calico tree.
Their wings were blue,
And they sang "Tilly-loo!"
Till away they flew;
And they never came back to me!
They never came back,
They never came back,
They never came back to me!

II
Calico jam,
The little fish swam
Over the Syllabub Sea.
He took off his hat
To the Sole and the Sprat,
And the Willeby-wat;
But he never came back to me!
He never came back,
He never came back,
He never came back to me!

continued

fold here

III

Calico ban,

The little Mice ran

To be ready in time for tea.

Flippity-flup,

They drank it all up,

And danced in the cup;

But they never came back to me!

They never came back,

They never came back,

They never came back to me!

IV

Calico drum,

The Grasshoppers come,

The Buttlerfly, Beetle, and Bee,

Over the ground,

Around and round,

With a hop and a bound;

But they never came back to me!

They never came back,

They never came back,

They never came back to me!

SUGGESTION: Assign children to four groups. Ask each group to practice one section and perform it for their classmates. Then ask them what *calico* or *calico pie* might be? Look up the word *calico* in the dictionary. Children may be able to infer its definition if they are familiar with calico cats. Have them speculate on why Edward Lear uses the word *calico* in the poem.

The Cat of Cats

by William Brighty Rands

I am the cat of cats. I am
The everlasting cat!
Cunning, and old, and sleek as jam,
The everlasting cat!
I hunt the vermin in the night—
The everlasting cat!
For I see best without the light—
The everlasting cat!

fold here

SUGGESTION: Children will enjoy this image of a cat. Underline or make a web of the words that describe the cat (*cunning, old, sleek as jam*). Ask the class what the poet means by *everlasting cat.* Now invite children to brainstorm new descriptive words for cats: e.g., *claws, whiskers,* and *curious.* Then help them compose additional lines in keeping with the poem's rhyming scheme.

Caterpillar

by Christina Rossetti

Brown and furry

Caterpillar in a hurry,

Take your walk

To the shady leaf, or stalk,

Or what not,

Which may be the chosen spot.

No toad spy you,

Hovering bird of prey pass by you;

Spin and die,

To live again a butterfly.

SUGGESTION: Christina Rossetti's poem captures a caterpillar's transformation into a butterfly. Invite children to talk about the simple yet descriptive images. Then present this poem with others found in this volume, such as "The Butterfly," "Fuzzy Little Caterpillar," or "Little Arabella Miller."

The Centipede's Song

Forty thousand little legs,

Walking down the stairs.

Forty thousand little feet,

Walking down in pairs.

Crunching on the gravel,

Marching in the shade,

Sounding like an army

Of soldiers on parade.

How happy are the centipedes,

Who do not have a care,

Except to keep their thousands

Of boots in good repair.

SUGGESTION: Invite children to talk about how the poem helps them appreciate this insect by comparing the centipede's feet to people's feet. Then ask them to look at the word *centipede* and connect it to other words like *pedal*, *pedestrian*, *pedestal*, *cent*, and *century*. Have them talk about the parts of the words that look alike and also how they might be connected by meaning.

fold here

The Chickens

Said the first little chicken,
With a queer little squirm,
"I wish I could find
A fat little worm."

Said the next little chicken,
With an odd little shrug,
"I wish I could find
A fat little slug."

Said the third little chicken,
With a sharp little squeal,
"I wish I could find
Some nice yellow meal."

Said the fourth little chicken,
With a small sigh of grief,
"I wish I could find
A little green leaf."

Said the fifth little chicken,
With a faint little moan,
"I wish I could find
A wee gravel stone."

"Now, see here," said the mother,
From the green garden patch,
"If you want any breakfast,
Just come here and scratch."

SUGGESTION: As children become familiar with this poem, assign them different roles: e.g., the *first, second, third, fourth,* and *fifth little chicken* as well as *mother*. Ask those who are not assigned a character to act as narrators. Performers will need practice time to work with the language and to remember their parts. Now have the six partner groups perform their stanzas in poem order. Don't miss the chance to revisit this poem when children are learning about words with vowels and the letter *r*.

Choosing a Kitten

A black-nosed kitten will slumber all the day;

A white-nosed kitten is ever glad to play;

A yellow-nosed kitten will answer to your call;

And a gray-nosed kitten I like best of all.

SUGGESTION: Invite children to talk about their own pets: e.g., describe how they look or act, and tell how they adopted them. Children who don't have pets may talk about the pets they wish they had. Now ask children to write down their thoughts and then illustrate them.

fold here

The City Mouse and the Garden Mouse

by Christina Rossetti

The city mouse lives in a house; –

The garden mouse lives in a bower,

He's friendly with the frogs and toads,

And sees the pretty plants in flower.

The city mouse eats bread and cheese; –

The garden mouse eats what he can;

We will not grudge him seeds and stalks,

Poor little, timid, furry man.

SUGGESTION: Discuss words like *bower, grudge,* and *timid,* which children may not know. After they listen to the poem, ask children to make comparisons between the lives of the two very different mice. Invite them to expand their thinking by talking about what it may be like for people who live in a city versus those who live in the country: e.g., what do they have in common and what is unique to each setting. Pair this poem with Jan Brett's picture book *Town Mouse, Country Mouse* (1994) found in the *Fountas & Pinnell Classroom™ Interactive Read-Aloud Collection, Grade 2* (2018).

Clouds

White sheep, white sheep,

On a blue hill.

When the wind stops,

You all stand still.

When the wind blows,

You walk away slow.

White sheep, white sheep,

Where do you go?

SUGGESTION: Present this poem without the title as a riddle for the class to solve, and see if a discussion produces the answer: *Clouds*. Now explain how the poem's use of *white sheep* is a metaphor for clouds because a metaphor is "a way to use symbolic words to help make comparisons." What other metaphors can children think of for clouds? Take a trip outside and invite the class to look up at the clouds for inspiration—especially in their movement and changing shapes.

fold here

Cockles and Mussels

In Dublin's fair city
Where girls are so pretty,
'Twas there I first met with
Sweet Molly Malone.

She drove a wheelbarrow
Through streets broad and narrow,
Crying, "Cockles and mussels,
Alive, alive-o."

Alive, alive-o
Alive, alive-o
Crying, "Cockles and mussels,
Alive, alive-o."

She was a fishmonger,
But sure 'twas no wonder.
For so were her mother
And father before.

They drove their wheelbarrows
Through streets broad and narrow,
Crying, "Cockles and mussels,
Alive, alive-o."

Alive, alive-o
Alive, alive-o
Crying, "Cockles and mussels,
Alive, alive-o."

SUGGESTION: You may need to define unfamiliar or archaic language for children: e.g., a *fishmonger* is "someone who sells live shellfish on the city streets" and *'twas* means "it was." While reciting this poem, ask children to think about the rhythmic chant and how it serves as advertising. If children do not live near or have not visited a seacoast town, explain that a *fishmonger's* work is still common today in areas near wharves.

The Codfish

The codfish lays ten thousand eggs,

The homely hen lays one.

The codfish never cackles

To tell you what she's done.

And so we scorn the codfish,

While the humble hen we prize,

Which only goes to show you

That it pays to advertise.

SUGGESTION: Have children discuss what makes this poem funny and uncover the comparisons in it. *It pays to advertise* is a common saying, but the humor lies in the comparison of the hen's cackle to television and newspaper ads.

fold here

Color

by Christina Rossetti

What is pink? a rose is pink

By the fountain's brink.

What is red? a poppy's red

In its barley bed.

What is blue? the sky is blue

Where the clouds float through.

What is white? a swan is white

Sailing in the night.

What is yellow? pears are yellow,

Rich and ripe and mellow.

What is green? the grass is green,

With small flowers between.

What is violet? clouds are violet

In the summer twilight.

What is orange? why, an orange,

Just an orange!

SUGGESTION: When reading this poem together as a class, you may wish to divide children into two groups: one to ask the poem's questions (*What is pink?*) and one to answer them (*a rose is pink / By a fountain's brink*). After children are familiar with the poem, ask them to pair up to brainstorm other examples of things that are pink, red, blue, white, yellow, green, violet, and orange. Help them to rewrite color couplets: e.g., *What is white? the clouds are white / In the sky where I fly my kite.*

Combinations

A flea flew by a bee. The bee
To flee the flea flew by a fly.
The fly flew high to flee the bee
Who flew to flee the flea who flew
To flee the fly who now flew by.

The bee flew by the fly. The fly
To flee the bee flew by the flea.
The flea flew high to flee the fly
Who flew to flee the bee who flew
To flee the flea who now flew by.

The fly flew by the flea. The flea
To flee the fly flew by the bee.
The bee flew high to flee the flea
Who flew to flee the fly who flew
To flee the bee who now flew by.

continued

fold here

The flea flew by the fly. The fly

To flee the flea flew by the bee.

The bee flew high to flee the fly

Who flew to flee the flea who flew

To flee the bee who now flew by.

The fly flew by the bee. The bee

To flee the fly flew by the flea.

The flea flew high to flee the bee

Who flew to flee the fly who flew

To flee the flea who now flew by.

The bee flew by the flea. The flea

To flee the bee flew by the fly.

The fly flew high to flee the flea

Who flew to flee the bee who flew

To flee the fly who now flew by.

SUGGESTION: This tongue twister is a tough one, but the simple words make it easier for children to reread and practice. To start, display only the first verse on a pocket chart. Once children are familiar with the structure, substitute words into the repetitive pattern using new animal and action cards. After children have time to practice, give them a photocopy of the poem in its entirety. Invite them to practice reading the substitutions across all six stanzas.

The Cow

by Robert Louis Stevenson

The friendly cow, all red and white,

I love with all my heart:

She gives me cream with all her might,

To eat with apple-tart.

She wanders lowing here and there,

And yet she cannot stray,

All in the pleasant open air,

The pleasant light of day.

And blown by all the winds that pass

And wet with all the showers,

She walks among the meadow grass

And eats the meadow flowers.

© 2019 by Irene C. Fountas and Gay Su Pinnell from *Sing a Song of Poetry, Grade 2*. Portsmouth, NH: Heinemann. May be photocopied for classroom use only.

SUGGESTION: Invite groups of children to take turns reading each verse of this poem. Ask them what they know about cows. Though some may have never seen a cow in person, children may know that cows milk is for baby cows, or calves, but that it also gives us butter and cream. Explain that *lowing* is "the mooing sound a cow makes." There are many picture books about these animals: e.g., *The Cow Who Wouldn't Come Down* by Paul Johnson (1993) and *Cows in the Kitchen* by June Crebbin (1998).

fold here

Cradle Song

by Alfred, Lord Tennyson

What does little birdie say

In her nest at peep of day?

Let me fly, says little birdie,

Mother, let me fly away.

Birdie, rest a little longer,

Till thy little wings are stronger;

So she rests a little longer,

Then she flies away.

What does little baby say,

In her bed at peep of day?

Baby says, like little birdie,

Let me rise and fly away.

Baby, sleep a little longer,

Till the little limbs are stronger;

If she sleeps a little longer,

Baby too shall fly away.

© 2019 by Irene C. Fountas and Gay Su Pinnell from *Sing a Song of Poetry, Grade 2*. Portsmouth, NH: Heinemann. May be photocopied for classroom use only.

fold here

SUGGESTION: This poem is about growth and change. Help children understand why Tennyson is comparing a baby with a small bird. They may want to talk about how children and birds are alike but also how their growth cycles are different.

Curly Locks

Curly Locks, Curly Locks,

Will you be mine?

You shall not wash dishes,

Nor yet feed the swine,

But sit on a cushion

And sew a fine seam;

And feed upon strawberries,

Sugar, and cream.

SUGGESTION: Be sure children know that *locks* means "hair" and *swine* means "pigs." Invite children to talk about who they think the narrator is and what he or she is trying to say.

fold here

Daffy Down Dilly

Daffy Down Dilly

Has come to town,

In a yellow petticoat,

And a green gown.

SUGGESTION: Children will enjoy the simplicity of this poem but may need help to understand the metaphor. Discuss the daffodil as one of the signs of spring. If you have flowers in the classroom place the poem near them or on a window overlooking flowers outside.

December Leaves

by Kaye Starbird

The fallen leaves are cornflakes

That fill the lawn's wide dish,

And night and noon

The wind's a spoon

That stirs them with a swish.

The sky's a silver sifter,

A-sifting white and slow,

That gently shakes

On crisp brown flakes

The sugar known as snow.

fold here

SUGGESTION: Walk children through this poem's metaphor, inviting them to offer their own guesswork. Once they are familiar with the poem and its imagery, invite small groups of children to illustrate individual copies. Have them glue on green, gold, and orange *cornflake leaves*. (Make the leaves by mixing one or two tablespoons of rubbing alcohol and some food coloring in separate containers, adding cornflakes, and then closing and shaking the containers.) Finally, ask children to add silver glitter for the snow.

Denise Sees the Fleece

Denise sees the fleece,

Denise sees the fleas.

At least Denise could sneeze,

And feed and freeze the fleas.

SUGGESTION: This nonsense verse is enjoyable because of the juxtaposition of words that sound the same (or almost the same) but mean completely different things. After children know the poem, you may want to revisit it for examples of *-ee* and *-ea* words.

Do Your Ears Hang Low?

Do your ears hang low?

Do they wobble to and fro?

Can you tie them in a knot?

Can you tie them in a bow?

Can you throw them o'er your shoulder,

Like a Continental Soldier?

Do your ears hang low?

Do your ears hang high?

Do they reach up to the sky?

Do they wrinkle when they're wet?

Do they straighten when they're dry?

Can you wave them at your neighbor,

With an element of flavor?

Do your ears hang high?

continued

fold here

Do your ears hang wide?

Do they flap from side to side?

Do they wave in the breeze

From the slightest little sneeze?

Can you soar above the nation,

With a feeling of elation?

Do your ears hang wide?

Do your ears fall off

When you give a great big cough?

Do they lie there on the ground,

Or bounce up at every sound?

Can you stick them in your pocket,

Just like Davy Crockett?

Do your ears fall off?

ADDITIONAL VERSES:

Does your tongue hang down?	Does your nose hang low?	Do your eyes pop out?
Does it flop all around?	Does it wiggle to and fro?	Do they bounce all about?
Is it stringy at the bottom?	Can you flap it up and down,	Can you use them like a ball?
Is it curly at the top?	As you fly around the town?	Can you take them in and out?
Can you use it for a swatter?	Can you turn it up for sure,	Can they do the boogie woogie,
Can you use it for a blotter?	When you hear an awful bore?	Like they do in any movie?
Does your tongue hang down?	Does your nose hang low?	Do your eyes pop out?

SUGGESTION: A popular way to sing this song is to take one stanza and sing it over and over, speeding up each time until it is no longer possible to go faster. Alternatively, divide the class into four groups and assign each group one stanza to practice; assign the *ear* group just one of the four stanzas. Then invite each group to make up hand motions imitating its stanza's part of the body. Finally, ask the class to perform the poem, group by group.

Doctor Foster

Doctor Foster

Went to Gloucester

In a shower of rain.

He stepped in a puddle

Right up to his middle

And never went there again.

SUGGESTION: Be sure children know that *Gloucester,* though it may not look it, rhymes with *Foster.* Display this poem by a classroom window and recite it together on rainy days.

fold here

Donkey, Donkey

Donkey, donkey, old and gray,

Open your mouth and gently bray.

Lift your ears and blow your horn,

To wake the world this sleepy morn.

Gee up, donkey, to the fair.

What shall I buy when I get there?

A half-penny apple, a penny pear,

Gee up, donkey, to the fair.

Donkey, donkey, do not bray,

But mend your pace and trot away.

Indeed, the market's almost done,

My butter's melting in the sun.

SUGGESTION: Ask children to suggest actions to accompany the poem. They will enjoy opening their mouths to bray and blowing their pretend horns. Invite them to talk about how people long ago rode donkeys, mules, or horses to market and home again. Also explain that some people still do this. Children may understand *market* as "grocery store" and *fair* as "a carnival"; explain that, historically, these words were both used to describe a place people would go to sell and buy things. Now have children retell this poem in prose, noting the sequence of events.

The Donut Song

Oh, I ran around the corner,

And I ran around the block.

I ran right in to the baker's shop.

I grabbed me a donut

Right out of the grease,

And I handed the lady

A five-cent piece.

She looked at the nickel,

And she looked at me.

She said, "This nickel,

Is no good to me.

There's a hole in the nickel,

And it goes right through."

Said I, "There's a hole in the donut, too!

Thanks for the donut. Good-bye!"

SUGGESTION: Assign two children to perform the quoted parts, and invite the rest of the class to recite the role of narrator. Have them sing to the tune of "Turkey in the Straw." Alternatively, they can recite it as a rap song.

fold here

Doodle-lee-do

Please sing to me that sweet melody,

Called Doodle-lee-do-doodle-lee-do.

I like the rest, but the one I like best,

Goes Doodle-lee-do-doodle-lee-do.

It's the simplest thing, there isn't much to it.

All you gotta do is Doodle-lee-do it.

I like it so that wherever I go,

It's the Doodle-lee-doodle-lee-do.

Come on and Waddle-lee-atcha-waddle-lee-atcha,

Waddle-lee-o-waddle-lee-o.

Waddle-lee-atcha-waddle-lee-atcha,

Waddle-lee-o-waddle-lee-o.

It's the simplest thing, there isn't much to it.

All you gotta do is Doodle-lee-do it.

I like it so that wherever I go,

It's the Doodle-lee-doodle-lee-do.

© 2019 by Irene C. Fountas and Gay Su Pinnell from *Sing a Song of Poetry, Grade 2*. Portsmouth, NH: Heinemann. May be photocopied for classroom use only.

SUGGESTION: Hand movements compliment this funny song and help to carry its catchy rhythm. Invite children to snap their fingers on the three syllables of Doodle-lee and then clap once on each *do* of *Doodle-lee-do*. Have them do the same on *Waddle-lee-o*, respectively. On the *atcha* of *Waddle-lee-atcha*, ask children to clap twice for each syllable.

Down by the Bay

Down by the bay where the watermelons grow,
Back to my home I dare not go.
For if I do my mother will say,
"Did you ever see a pig dancing the jig?"
Down by the bay.

Down by the bay where the watermelons grow,
Back to my home I dare not go.
For if I do my mother will say,
"Did you ever see a whale with a polka-dot tail?"
Down by the bay.

Down by the bay where the watermelons grow,
Back to my home I dare not go.
For if I do my mother will say,
"Did you ever see a bear combing his hair?"
Down by the bay.

Down by the bay where the watermelons grow,
Back to my home I dare not go.
For if I do my mother will say,
"Did you ever see a moose kissing a goose?"
Down by the bay.

Down by the bay where the watermelons grow,
Back to my home I dare not go.
For if I do my mother will say,
"Did you ever see a bee with a sunburned knee?"
Down by the bay.

SUGGESTION: Invite children to recite this poem rapidly, clapping their hands or tapping their feet to keep—and then gradually hasten—the beat. Then ask them to create new verses with the same structure by revising each stanza's fourth line: e.g., *"Did you ever see a snake eating cake?"*

fold here

Elephant

The elephant carries a great big trunk.

She never packs it with her clothes.

It has no lock and it has no key,

But she takes it wherever she goes.

fold here

SUGGESTION: This short poem plays on the word *trunk*. Explain to children the meaning of *pun* or *play on words*. Invite them to draw cartoons illustrating this rhyme to ensure the double meaning of the word will stick in their heads. Then ask children if they can think of a different word whose double meaning can describe a new animal: e.g., a kangaroo's joey whose name is anything but Joey. Alternatively, consider having children play with words that sound alike but carry different meanings: e.g., a *tale* as in a story versus an animal's *tail*. Remember to return this poem when working on words with multiple meanings.

Eletelephony

by Laura E. Richards

Once there was an elephant,

Who tried to use the telephant—

No! No! I mean an elephone

Who tried to use the telephone—

(Dear me! I am not certain quite

That even now I've got it right.)

Howe'er it was, he got his trunk

Entangled in the telephunk;

The more he tried to get it free,

The louder buzzed the telephee—

(I fear I'd better drop the song

Of elephop and telephong!)

SUGGESTION: Invite children to practice reciting this poem until they are comfortable with its word play. Then ask them to illustrate the poem, perhaps by drawing an elephant tangled in a telephone cord. Children will probably see the cordless phone as a solution. After they know the poem, make a list of all the words and the connections between word parts.

fold here

Eye Rhymes

You see me, I see you.

Your eyes are blue. Mine are, too.

Your eyes are big and round and brown.

They must be the prettiest eyes in town.

When I look at you, know what I see?

Eyes as green as green can be.

Blue eyes, green eyes,

Brown eyes, hey.

Your eyes are gray,

And I like them that way.

SUGGESTION: Read the poem aloud as a class. Then instruct the class to recite the poem again, but this time ask each child to only say aloud the verse that best describes him or herself. Children will enjoy finding out who will recite which verse. Afterwards, invite children to partner up. Partners may or may not share the same eye color. invite partners to draw portraits of each other to appreciate different eye color as well as other attributes.

A Fairy Went A-marketing

by Rose Fyleman

A fairy went a-marketing—

She bought a little fish;

She put it a crystal bowl

Upon a golden dish.

An hour she sat in wonderment

And watched its silver gleam,

And then she gently took it up

And slipped it in a stream.

A fairy went a-marketing—

She bought a colored bird;

It sang the sweetest, shrillest song

That ever she had heard.

She sat beside the painted cage

And listened half the day.

And then she opened wide the door

And let it fly away.

continued

fold here

A fairy went a-marketing—

She bought a winter gown

All stitched about with gossamer

And lined with thistledown.

She wore it all afternoon

With prancing and delight,

then gave it to a little frog

To keep him warm at night.

A fairy went a-marketing—

She bought a gentle mouse

To take her tiny messages,

and keep her tiny house.

All day she kept its busy feet

Pit-patting to and fro,

And then she kissed its silken ears,

Thanked it, and let it go.

SUGGESTION: This poem tells a story about buying different things (living and nonliving) to look at or to use before letting them go. Invite children to tell the poem in prose; this will help them to highlight contrasts between story poems and story prose. Then ask the class to talk about why the fairy let each living thing go. Lead the discussion so that children consider why some animals cannot be released into the wild: e.g., they are domesticated.

Ferry Me Across the Water

by Christina Rossetti

"Ferry me across the water,

Do, boatman, do."

"If you've a penny in your purse

I'll ferry you."

"I have a penny in my purse,

And my eyes are blue;

So ferry me across the water,

Do, boatman, do."

"Step into my ferry-boat,

Be they black or blue,

And for the penny in your purse

I'll ferry you."

SUGGESTION: Divide children into two groups when reciting this poem: one to narrate the passenger and one to narrate the boatman. Alternatively, ask two children to perform as the passenger and boatman while the rest of the class recites the poem. For example, the child playing the passenger can pretend to pay the boatman with a penny. The boatman can pretend to paddle a make-believe boat. Also, children may need you to define the word *ferry* if they cannot infer its meaning based on the actions in the poem.

fold here

Fiddle-i-fee

I had a cat and my cat pleased me.
I fed my cat under yonder tree.
Cat plays fiddle-i-fee.

I had a duck and my duck pleased me.
I fed my duck under yonder tree.
Duck plays quaa-quaa, quaa-quaa,
Cat plays fiddle-i-fee.

I had a goose and my goose pleased me.
I fed my goose under yonder tree.
Goose plays hum-sum, hum-sum,
Duck plays quaa-quaa, quaa-quaa,
Cat plays fiddle-i-fee.

ADDITIONAL VERSES:

I had a hen and my hen pleased me.
I fed my hen under yonder tree.
Hen plays chimmy-chuck, chimmy-chuck,
etc.

I had a pig and my pig pleased me.
I fed my pig under yonder tree.
Pig plays griffy-griffy, griffy-griffy,
etc.

I had a cow and my cow pleased me.
I fed my cow under yonder tree.
Cow plays strum-strum, strum-strum,
etc.

I had a horse and my horse pleased me.
I fed my horse under yonder tree.
Horse plays dub-ub, dub-ub,
etc.

I had a dog and my dog pleased me.
I fed my dog under yonder tree.
Dog plays clickity-clack, clickity-clack,
etc.

I had a sheep and my sheep pleased me.
I fed my sheep under yonder tree.
Sheep plays shake-shake, shake-shake,
etc.

fold here

SUGGESTION: The numerous verses and cumulative structure of this poem may necessitate presenting it on chart paper or in a pocket chart to help children learn and remember it. Alternatively, divide the class into nine groups—one for each verse. Ask children to practice reading their group's verse, and encourage them to create accompanying hand or body movements. Some may also feel inspired to assign roles: e.g., narrator, *yonder tree*, and their stanza's respective animal. Now have each group perform and pantomime its portion of the poem.

Firefighters

Up onto their loud, loud truck

The firefighters climb,

They're in an awful hurry,

They move in quick, quick time.

They're going to put out a fire,

Help is on the way.

They'll get there with their water hose

And spray and spray and spray.

SUGGESTION: Children will love to enact the part of firefighters. Ask them to add their own actions or movements as they recite. Pair this poem with Chris Demarest's alphabet book *Firefighters A to Z* (2000).

fold here

Five Cream Buns

Five cream buns in Teddy's shop,

Teddy's shop, Teddy's shop,

Five cream buns in Teddy's shop,

Round and fat with a cherry on top.

Along came _____,

Hungry one day,

She bought a cream bun

And took it away.

ADDITIONAL VERSES:

Four cream buns in Teddy's shop . . .

Three cream buns in Teddy's shop . . .

Two cream buns in Teddy's shop . . .

One cream bun in Teddy's shop . . .

No cream buns in Teddy's shop . . .

SUGGESTION: Make copies of this countdown poem and invite children to write in their own names. *Five Cream Buns and Five Currant Buns* (see next page) are variations of each other. Be sure to call attention to this and to use the opportunity to discuss *variations*. Have children compare the poems' overall cadence and syllables across lines. Working with a partner, or in small groups, encourage the class to create their own variations. Using the countdown structure of this poem as a model, partners or groups can create separate stanzas and then recite their versions aloud for the whole class to enjoy.

Five Currant Buns

Five currant buns in the baker's shop,
Big and round with some sugar on the top.
Along came Tom with a penny to pay,
Who bought a currant bun and took it right away.

Four currant buns in the baker's shop,
Big and round with some sugar on the top.
Along came Tom with a penny to pay,
Who bought a currant bun and took it right away.

Three currant buns in the baker's shop,
Big and round with some sugar on the top.
Along came Tom with a penny to pay,
Who bought a currant bun and took it right away.

Two currant buns in the baker's shop,
Big and round with some sugar on the top.
Along came Tom with a penny to pay,
Who bought a currant bun and took it right away.

One currant bun in the baker's shop,
Big and round with some sugar on the top.
Along came Tom with a penny to pay,
Who bought a currant bun and took it right away.

No currant buns in the baker's shop,
Big and round with some sugar on the top.
No one came with a penny to pay.
So close the baker's shop and have a baking day.

SUGGESTION: As you compare this variation to the previous poem, *Five Cream Buns*, note and discuss the difference in line presentation. For example, *Five Cream Buns* is presented in eight-line stanzas, whereas this one is presented in four-line stanzas. Ask children to compare the poems, investigate the differences, and choose the model they'd like to use as they create new verses. Also, invite children to replace *currant bun* with a favorite sweet treat and the place where they would logically buy this sweet treat: e.g., *ice cream* at the *ice cream parlor* or *ice cream truck*.

fold here

Five Fat Turkeys

Five fat turkeys are we.

We slept all night in a tree.

When the cook came around,

We couldn't be found.

So, that's why we're here, you see.

ACTIONS:

Five fat turkeys are we. [*hold up five fingers*]

We slept all night in a tree. [*put head to the side as if sleeping*]

When the cook came around,

We couldn't be found. [*shake head no*]

So, that's why we're here, you see. [*point to selves*]

fold here

SUGGESTION: Children may already know this poem and the simple actions that accompany it. It is a great poem to revisit when reviewing contractions.

Five Little Owls

Five little owls in an old elm tree,

Fluffy and puffy as owls could be,

Blinking and winking with big round eyes

At the big round moon that hung in the skies:

As I passed beneath, I could hear one say,

"There'll be mouse for supper, there will, today!"

Then all of them hooted, "Tu-whit, tu-whoo!

Yes, mouse for supper, hoo-hoo, hoo-hoo!"

ADDITIONAL VERSES:

Four little owls in an old elm tree . . .

Three little owls in an old elm tree . . .

Two little owls in an old elm tree . . .

One little owl in an old elm tree . . .

No little owls in an old elm tree . . .

SUGGESTION: When reciting this poem as a class, consider varying the number of owls and counting down or up accordingly. For each differing verse, invite a new child to recite the sixth line. This poem may inspire a discussion about how owls are nocturnal creatures who like to hunt small rodents, such as mice. Ask children if they can think of any other nocturnal animals, or perhaps animals who are more or less active during select parts of the year and the reasons why (e.g., bears hibernate in the winter).

fold here

Five Waiting Pumpkins

Five little pumpkins growing on a vine,

First one said, "It's time to shine!"

Second one said, "I love the fall!"

Third one said, "I'm round as a ball!"

Fourth one said, "I want to be a pie!"

Fifth one said, "Let's say good-bye!"

"Good-bye!" said one.

"Adios!" said two.

"Au revoir!" said three.

"Ciao!" said four.

"Aloha!" said five.

And five little pumpkins were picked that day!

SUGGESTION: Introduce this poem in the fall when it's time to harvest pumpkins. Talk about what it means to harvest things that grow and how much hard work goes in between sowing and harvesting. Reciting countdown poems like this one adds suspense; children are eager to find out what the next pumpkin will say as it follows the rhyming pattern. The pumpkins in this rhyme speak different languages. Invite children to come up with other ways to say good-bye—in English or in a language not yet said.

Fooba Wooba, John

Saw a flea kick a tree,
Fooba wooba, fooba wooba,
Saw a flea kick a tree,
Fooba wooba, John.
Saw a flea kick a tree,
In the middle of the sea,
Hey, John, ho, John,
Fooba wooba, John.

Saw a crow flying low,
Fooba wooba, fooba wooba,
Saw a crow flying low,
Fooba wooba, John.
Saw a crow flying low,
Miles and miles beneath the snow,
Hey, John, ho, John,
Fooba wooba, John.

Saw a bug give a shrug,
Fooba wooba, fooba wooba,
Saw a bug give a shrug,
Fooba wooba, John.
Saw a bug give a shrug,
In the middle of the rug,
Hey, John, ho, John,
Fooba wooba, John.

continued

Saw a whale chase a snail,
Fooba wooba, fooba wooba,
Saw a whale chase a snail,
Fooba wooba, John.
Saw a whale chase a snail,
All around a water pail,
Hey, John, ho, John,
Fooba wooba, John.

Saw two geese making cheese,
Fooba wooba, fooba wooba,
Saw two geese making cheese,
Fooba wooba, John.
Saw two geese making cheese,
One would hold and the other would squeeze,
Hey, John, ho, John,
Fooba wooba, John.

Saw a mule teaching school,
Fooba wooba, fooba wooba,
Saw a mule teaching school,
Fooba wooba, John.
Saw a mule teaching school,
To some bullfrogs in the pool,
Hey, John, ho, John,
Fooba wooba, John.

fold here

SUGGESTION: This is an old camp song. Invite children to sing and act out the nonsense words using hand or body movements. Encourage them to also replace *John* with the names of classmates. Add on the following verses or create new ones using a different sense (e.g., *heard a* or *smelled a*): *Saw a bee off to sea… With his fiddle across his knee. / Saw a bear scratch his ear… Wonderin' what we're doin' here. / Heard a cow say meow… And then take a little bow.*

Foreign Lands

by Robert Louis Stevenson

Up into the cherry tree
Who should climb but little me?
I held the trunk with both my hands
And looked abroad in foreign lands.

I saw the next door garden lie,
Adorned with flowers, before my eye,
And many pleasant places more
That I had never seen before.

I saw the dimpling river pass
And be the sky's blue looking-glass;
The dusty roads go up and down
With people tramping in to town.

If I could find a higher tree
Farther and farther I should see,
To where the grown-up river slips
Into the sea among the ships,

To where the road on either hand
Lead onward into fairy land,
Where all the children dine at five,
And all the playthings come alive.

© 2019 by Irene C. Fountas and Gay Su Pinnell from *Sing a Song of Poetry, Grade 2*. Portsmouth, NH: Heinemann. May be photocopied for classroom use only.

SUGGESTION: The narrator enjoys climbing trees and daydreams about being an explorer. Ask children to talk about their favorite outdoor activities. Do they daydream and play pretend like the narrator? If yes, about what? Together as a class, create a list of favorite outdoor activities. Then, also as a class, write a couplet about one of the outdoor activities: e.g., *Up and up and up I swing / Flying high like a bird with wings.* Invite children to illustrate the class' couplet—or a different outdoor activity that they favor.

fold here

Found a Peanut

Found a peanut, found a peanut,
Found a peanut last night.
Last night I found a peanut,
Found a peanut last night.

Cracked it open, cracked it open,
Cracked it open last night.
Last night I cracked it open,
Cracked it open last night.

It was rotten, it was rotten,
It was rotten last night.
Last night it was rotten,
It was rotten last night.

Ate it anyway, ate it anyway,
Ate it anyway last night.
Last night ate it anyway,
Ate it anyway last night.

Got a tummy ache, got a tummy ache,
Got a tummy ache last night.
Last night got a tummy ache,
Got a tummy ache last night.

fold here

SUGGESTION: Invite children to sing this song to the tune of "Clementine." The simple repetitive structure makes it easy for them to create additional verses; any phrase with three or four syllables will work. Point out the poem's storytelling nature. Encourage children to continue the story as they make up new verses: e.g., *Called the Doctor...*, *Had an operation...*, *Was a Dream...*, and *Then I Woke Up....*

The Fox Went Out on a Chilly Night

The fox went out on a chilly night,

He called to the moon to give him light.

For he'd many a mile to go that night

Before he'd reach the town-o, town-o, town-o.

He'd many a mile to go that night

Before he'd reach the town-o.

SUGGESTION: Use this old story song for line-up at the end of the school day. You'll find it on many CDs and in many picture books, such as *The Fox Went Out on a Chilly Night: An Old Song* by Peter Spier (1961).

fold here

Frog Went A-courtin'

Frog went a-courtin' and he did ride.
Uh-huh, uh-huh.
Frog went a-courtin' and he did ride
With a sword and scabbard by his side.
Uh-huh, uh-huh.

He rode up to Miss Mousie's den.
Uh-huh, uh-huh.
He rode up to Miss Mousie's den,
Said, "Please, Miss Mousie, won't you let me in?"
Uh-huh, uh-huh.

"First I must ask my Uncle Rat."
Uh-huh, uh-huh.
"First I must ask my Uncle Rat,
And see what he will say to that."
Uh-huh, uh-huh.

ADDITIONAL VERSES:

"Miss Mousie, won't you marry me?"
Uh-huh, uh-huh.
"Miss Mousie, won't you marry me
Way down under the apple tree?"
Uh-huh, uh-huh.

"Where will the wedding supper be?"
Uh-huh, uh-huh.
"Where will the wedding supper be?
Under the same old apple tree?"
Uh-huh, uh-huh.

The first to come was a bumblebee.
Uh-huh, uh-huh.
The first to come was a bumblebee
With a big bass fiddle on his knee.
Uh-huh, uh-huh.

The last to come was a mockingbird.
Uh-huh, uh-huh.
The last to come was a mockingbird
Who said, "This marriage is absurd."
Uh-huh, uh-huh.

SUGGESTION: After children are familiar with the words, invite them to work in small groups, each practicing a stanza to be performed in front of the class. This song lends itself to making a class book or individual books with a stanza on each page. Children will enjoy drawing detailed illustrations for the scenes. John Langstaff retells this story in the Caldecott Medal award-winning picture book *Frog Went A-courtin'* (1955), as well as on his CD *Songs for Singing Children* (1996).

Fuzzy Little Caterpillar

Fuzzy little caterpillar,

Crawling, crawling on the ground,

Fuzzy little caterpillar,

Nowhere, nowhere to be found,

Though we've looked and looked and hunted,

Everywhere around!

When the little caterpillar

Found his furry coat too tight,

Then a snug cocoon he made him,

Spun of silk so soft and light,

Rolled himself away within it—

Slept there day and night.

See how this cocoon is stirring—

Now a little head we spy.

What! Is this our caterpillar,

Spreading gorgeous wings to dry?

Soon the free and happy creature

Flutters gaily by.

SUGGESTION: After children have listened to this poem and internalized the words, invite them to perform finger play actions. Have them wiggle their thumbs to show the caterpillar crawling and then hide their thumbs (caterpillars) in a fist (cocoon) for the first two verses. For the third verse, ask children to cross their thumbs and spread their fingers to show the butterfly drying its wings. Finally, they can wiggle their fingers to show the fluttering creatures.

fold here

The Goat

There was a man—now please take note—

There was a man who had a goat.

He loved that goat—indeed he did—

He loved that goat just like a kid.

One day that goat felt frisky and fine,

Ate three red shirts from off the line.

The man, he grabbed him by the back

And tied him to a railroad track.

But when the train drove into sight,

The goat grew pale and green with fright.

He heaved a sigh as if in pain,

Coughed up those shirts, and flagged the train.

SUGGESTION: This is often presented as an echo song with a leader reciting one line at a time and the group repeating each line. Discuss how to *flag* something means "to stop it." Also talk about how the poem is not realistic; a goat in this predicament could not flag a train in time to stop it. Then ask children about the poem's *moral*, or its "message about right and wrong": e.g., was it right of the man to react like he did after the goat ate his shirts? Sometimes it's fun to pretend, but only if we know it's make-believe.

Going on a Bear Hunt

Would you like to go on a bear hunt?
Okay—all right—come on—let's go!
Open the gate—close the gate. (*clap hands*)

Coming to a bridge—can't go over it—can't go under it.
Let's cross it. (*march in place*)

Coming to a river—can't go over it—can't go under it.
Let's swim it. (*make swimming motions*)

Coming to a tree—can't go over it—can't go under it.
Let's climb it. (*make climbing-up motions*)

No bears! (*make climbing-down motions*)

Coming to a wheat field—can't go over it—can't go under it.
Let's go through it! (*rub palms together to make swishing noise*)

Oh! Oh! I see a cave—it's dark in here. (*cover eyes*)
I see two eyes—I feel something furry. (*reach out hand*)

It's a bear!
Let's go home! (*run in place*)

(*quickly repeat the above actions in reverse order*)

Slam the gate! (*clap hands*)
We made it!

SUGGESTION: This poem is a favorite action rhyme; children will enjoy having a reproduced version to reference while reciting the words and performing each action. They will also enjoy gluing verses into an eight-page book. After children learn the poem and its actions—both forward and in reverse—show them the picture book *We're Going on a Bear Hunt* written by Michael Rosen (1989). Invite them to compare versions. Then ask them to illustrate the poem's verses in their eight-page books, using the picture book as inspiration.

fold here

Gold Ships

There are gold ships.

There are silver ships.

But there's no ship

Like a friendship.

SUGGESTION: Children will enjoy exploring this poem's play on words. The reference to *gold* and *silver ships* may make them think of the classic song "Make New Friends" (also in this volume): *Make new friends, / but keep the old. / One is silver, / and other gold.* Ask children what *gold* and *silver* descriptions mean in both poems. Then invite them to talk about and create new verses using a similar play on words.

Golden Slumbers

Golden slumbers kiss your eyes,

Smiles awake you when you rise.

Sleep, pretty baby, do not cry,

And I will sing a lullaby.

Rock then, rock then, lullaby.

Care is heavy, therefore sleep you,

You are care, and care must keep you.

Sleep, pretty baby, do not cry,

And I will sing a lullaby.

Rock then, rock then, lullaby.

SUGGESTION: Divide the class into two groups. Invite one group to recite the first verse while the other group hums softly in the background. Now ask groups to switch roles for the second verse. After children are familiar with the poem, ask them to talk about what *golden slumbers* are and what it means when they *kiss...eyes*. Then ask children what the poet means by *care is heavy* and *You are care*, and *care must keep you.*

fold here

Good, Better, Best

Good, better, best,

Never let it rest,

Till your good is better

And your better, best.

© 2019 by Irene C. Fountas and Gay Su Pinnell from *Sing a Song of Poetry, Grade 2*. Portsmouth, NH: Heinemann. May be photocopied for classroom use only.

SUGGESTION: This poem's moral lesson is a good motto for children. Invite them to talk about its message. Remind children that best is not the same as perfect: that everyone's best is different and this is okay. Then post a copy of the poem in the classroom to remind children to practice being their best selves—not the best version of others.

Good Morning, Merry Sunshine!

Good morning, merry sunshine!

How did you wake so soon?

You've scared the little stars away,

And shined away the moon.

I saw you go to sleep last night

Before I stopped my playing.

How did you get way over there,

And where have you been staying?

I never go to sleep, dear one,

I just go 'round to see

My little children of the

East who rise and watch for me.

I waken all the birds and bees

And flowers on my way.

And now come back to see the child

Who stayed out late to play.

© 2019 by Irene C. Fountas and Gay Su Pinnell from *Sing a Song of Poetry, Grade 2*. Portsmouth, NH: Heinemann. May be photocopied for classroom use only.

SUGGESTION: This poem is a good example of personification. It may take children a while to figure out the real meaning of the poem. Enjoy the language together and talk about how the sun, moon, and stars are described like people.

fold here

The Greedy Man

The greedy man is he who sits

And bites bits out of plates,

Or else takes up a calendar

And gobbles all the dates.

© 2019 by Irene C. Fountas and Gay Su Pinnell from *Sing a Song of Poetry, Grade 2*. Portsmouth, NH: Heinemann. May be photocopied for classroom use only.

SUGGESTION: Children will enjoy reciting the poem while pretending to be the greedy man who *bites bits out of plates* and *gobbles all the dates* in the calendar. Invite them to create additional silly lines or verses.

The Greengrocer's Love Song

Do you carrot all for me?

My heart beets for you.

With your turnip nose

And your radish face

You are a peach.

If we cantaloupe

Lettuce marry.

Weed make a swell pear.

SUGGESTION: This poem plays with language in a way children will enjoy. They may need help recognizing how a word's spelling and its sounds can playfully represent a new word or message: e.g., *If we cantaloupe* looks a little like, sounds like, and translates to *If we can't elope*. After children are familiar with the poem's use of word play, divide them into groups and ask each to try creating new word plays.

fold here

Gregory Griggs

Gregory Griggs, Gregory Griggs,

Had twenty-seven different wigs.

He wore them up, he wore them down,

To please the people of the town.

He wore them east, he wore them west,

But he never could tell which he loved the best.

fold here

SUGGESTION: Children will enjoy reciting the poem to its infectious beat. After they are familiar with the poem, ask them to brainstorm why Greggory Griggs *had twenty-seven different wigs*. Then invite them to illustrate the poem, drawing in their answers: e.g., he wore the wigs for a fashion show. Collect children's drawings and display them as a mural on the classroom wall.

Happy Thought

by Robert Louis Stevenson

The world is so full

Of a number of things,

I'm sure we should all

Be as happy as kings.

SUGGESTION: After enjoying the poem together, ask children if they are familiar with the role of happy thoughts in the classic story *Peter Pan* by J.M. Barrie (1911). If not, take a moment to explain; maybe even read a passage. Then invite children to brainstorm their own happy thoughts. Afterwards, record their happy thoughts on chart paper. Or, alternatively, ask children to write down and illustrate their happy thoughts. Then display them on the classroom wall.

fold here

Hickety, Pickety

Hickety, pickety, my black hen.

She lays eggs for gentlemen.

Sometimes nine,

And sometimes ten.

Hickety, pickety, my black hen.

fold here

SUGGESTION: This poem's rhythm is infectious; it's hard to get the words out of your head. Ask children why they think this is so. Be sure to revisit this poem when discussing compound words.

Higgledy, Piggledy, See How They Run

by Kate Greenaway

Higgledy, piggledy, see how they run!

Hopperty, popperty! what is the fun?

Has the sun or the moon tumbled into the sea?

What is the matter, now? Pray tell it me!

Higgledy, piggledy, how can I tell?

Hopperty, popperty! hark the bell!

The rats and the mice even scamper away;

Who can say what may not happen to-day?

SUGGESTION: This poem alludes to a dark, unknown occurrence. What is it? What role does the *bell* play? And where is it? Show children Kate Greenaway's original illustration from *Under the Window* (1878) to help them decipher what's happening in the poem. The book is public domain and available online.

fold here

The Hobbyhorse

I had a little hobbyhorse,

And it was dapple gray.

Its head was made of pea-straw,

Its tail was made of hay.

I sold it to an old woman

For a dollar bill.

And I'll not sing my song again

Till everything is still.

SUGGESTION: This is a fun poem to recite around the circle—one child reciting one line at a time. Alternatively, divide the class into groups of eight, and assign each group one line; with groups of four, assign lines one and five; two and six; etc. With practice, children will undoubtedly increase the pace and have fun making it a line-by-line race around the circle or between groups. Afterward, have them work to keep the rhythm and cadence of the performance smooth—almost as if one person was reciting. Revisit this poem when children are working with vowel sounds represented by different patterns in words (*a–e, ay, ai*).

The House That Jack Built

This is the house that Jack built.

This is the malt
That lay in the house that Jack built.

This is the rat,
That ate the malt,
That lay in the house that Jack built.

This is the cat,
That killed the rat,
That ate the malt,
That lay in the house that Jack built.

This is the dog,
That worried the cat,
That killed the rat,
That ate the malt,
That lay in the house that Jack built.

This is the cow with the crumpled horn,
That tossed the dog,
That worried the cat,
That killed the rat,
That ate the malt,
That lay in the house that Jack built.

continued

© 2019 by Irene C. Fountas and Gay Su Pinnell from *Sing a Song of Poetry, Grade 2*. Portsmouth, NH: Heinemann. May be photocopied for classroom use only.

fold here

This is the maiden all forlorn,
That milked the cow with the crumpled horn,
That tossed the dog,
That worried the cat,
That killed the rat,
That ate the malt,
That lay in the house that Jack built.

This is the man all tattered and torn,
That kissed the maiden all forlorn,
That milked the cow with the crumpled horn,
That tossed the dog,
That worried the cat,
That killed the rat,
That ate the malt,
That lay in the house that Jack built.

This is the leader all shaven and shorn,
That married the man all tattered and torn,
That kissed the maiden all forlorn,
That milked the cow with the crumpled horn,
That tossed the dog,
That worried the cat,
That killed the rat,
That ate the malt,
That lay in the house that Jack built.

continued

fold here

This is the rooster that crowed in the morn,

That woke the leader all shaven and shorn,

That married the man all tattered and torn,

That kissed the maiden all forlorn,

That milked the cow with the crumpled horn,

That tossed the dog,

That worried the cat,

That killed the rat,

That ate the malt,

That lay in the house that Jack built.

This is the farmer sowing his corn,

That kept the rooster that crowed in the morn,

That woke the leader all shaven and shorn,

That married the man all tattered and torn,

That kissed the maiden all forlorn,

That milked the cow with the crumpled horn,

That tossed the dog,

That worried the cat,

That killed the rat,

That ate the malt,

That lay in the house that Jack built.

SUGGESTION: This classic story poem is cumulative. The repeating lines in each stanza help children learn the words. Explain that *malt* is "grain" and that *forlorn* means "sad, lonely, or without." Invite children to brainstorm their own cumulative verses inspired by the poem's example: e.g., *This is the castle that Maria built.*

fold here

How Many Miles to Babylon?

How many miles to Babylon?

Threescore miles and ten.

Can I get there by candlelight?

Yes, and back again.

If your heels are nimble and light,

You may get there by candlelight.

fold here

SUGGESTION: Invite children to talk about this poem's mood. Why might they whisper or recite its lines in hushed tones? Then ask them where Babylon is, how many miles are *threescore and ten*, and what *candlelight* means in the context of the poem (it means "twilight" or "the time for lighting candles").

How Much Wood Would a Woodchuck Chuck

How much wood would a woodchuck chuck

If a woodchuck could chuck wood?

He would chuck as much wood as a woodchuck would chuck,

If a woodchuck could chuck wood.

SUGGESTION: Ask children if they know what a *woodchuck* is. You may need to explain what this animal is and its habits. Children will need to know in order to act like woodchucks while reciting this tricky tongue twister. Like any tongue twister, this poem is fun to say aloud, especially as children practice reciting it faster and faster. Offer a printed version to help them learn the words.

fold here

Humpty Dumpty's Song

by Lewis Caroll

In winter, when the fields are white,
I sing this song for your delight—

In spring, when woods are getting green,
I'll try and tell you what I mean:

In summer, when the days are long,
Perhaps you'll understand the song:

In autumn, when the leaves are brown,
Take pen and ink, and write it down.

I sent a message to the fish:
I told them, "This is what I wish."

The little fishes of the sea,
They sent an answer back to me.

The little fishes' answer was
"We cannot do it, Sir, because—"

I sent to them again to say,
"It will be better to obey."

The fishes answered, with a grin,
"Why, what a temper you are in!"

continued

fold here

124

I told them once, I told them twice:
They would not listen to advice.

I took a kettle large and new,
Fit for the deed I had to do.

My heart went hop, my heart went thump:
I filled the kettle at the pump.

Then some one came to me and said,
"The little fishes are in bed."

I said to him, I said it plain,
"Then you must wake them up again."

I said it very loud and clear:
I went and shouted in his ear.

But he was very stiff and proud:
He said, "You needn't shout so loud!"

And he was very proud and stiff:
He said, "I'd go and wake them, if—"

I took a corkscrew from the shelf:
I went to wake them up myself.

And when I found the door was locked,
I pulled and pushed and kicked and knocked.

And when I found the door was shut
I tried to turn the handle, but—

© 2019 by Irene C. Fountas and Gay Su Pinnell from *Sing a Song of Poetry, Grade 2*. Portsmouth, NH: Heinemann. May be photocopied for classroom use only.

SUGGESTION: Children will enjoy reading this classic nonsense poem from Lewis Carroll's *Through the Looking-Glass and What Alice Found There* (1871). Ask them to talk about how the poem's ending is different from other poems they have read. Divide children into groups and invite each to make up a final, silly stanza that concludes the poem. To help guide their creations, list different sets of familiar, rhyming words from which children can choose. Then have each group share its work with the rest of the class.

I Don't Suppose

I don't suppose

A lobster knows

The proper way

To blow his nose,

Or else perhaps

Beneath the seas

They have no need

to sniff and sneeze.

SUGGESTION: What a silly image: a lobster blowing his nose! Invite children to adapt the poem by adding their own silly actions: e.g., *blink her eyes*, *clap his claws*, or *scratch her shell*. They may also wish to tweak the last two lines accordingly. It is also a great poem to revisit when children are focusing on long /o/ and long /e/.

I Hear Thunder

I hear thunder, I hear thunder,

Hark don't you? Hark don't you?

Pitter patter raindrops, pitter patter raindrops,

I'm wet through, so are you!

I see blue skies, I see blue skies,

Way up high, way up high.

Hurry up the sunshine, hurry up the sunshine,

We'll soon dry, we'll soon dry.

SUGGESTION: Teach children to sing the rhyme to the tune of "Are You Sleeping (Frère Jacques)?" There are many weather-related verses in this volume: e.g., "Whether the Weather," "If All the Little Raindrops," and "Jack Frost." Consider pairing them with this poem for a weather poetry unit.

fold here

I Like Silver

I like silver.
I like brass.
I like looking
In the looking glass.

I like rubies.
I like pearls.
I like wearing
My hair in curls.

I like earrings.
I like clothes.
I like wearing
My hair in rows.

I like baseball.
I like bats.
I like wearing
Baseball hats.

SUGGESTION: Invite children to create new verses with the same simple "I like…" rhythm and pattern. Then ask them to illustrate their work.

I Live in the City

I live in the city, yes I do,
I live in the city, yes I do,
I live in the city, yes I do,
Made by human hands.

Black hands, white hands, tan and brown
All together built this town,
Black hands, white hands, tan and brown
All together make the wheels go 'round.

Black hands, brown hands, tan and white
Built the buildings tall and bright,
Black hands, brown hands, tan and white
Filled them all with shining light.

Black hands, white hands, brown and tan
Milled the flour and cleaned the pan,
Black hands, white hands, brown and tan
The working woman and the working man.

I live in the city, yes I do,
I live in the city, yes I do,
I live in the city, yes I do,
Made by human hands.

SUGGESTION: Invite children to talk about why the poet writes about different colored hands. Then randomly divide children into three groups and assign one of the three middle stanzas to each group. After children learn their respective verses, invite them to recite the poem as a class. Ask children how the first lines in the middle stanzas differ (the colors are listed in different orders to change the end-of-line rhyme). Now invite the class to create a fourth middle verse. Have children order the first line so that the color *black* is the end-of-line rhyme.

I Never Saw a Purple Cow

by Gelett Burgess

I never saw a purple cow.

I never hope to see one.

But I can tell you anyhow

I'd rather see than be one.

SUGGESTION: Children will enjoy this nonsense verse. Invite them to make up their own: e.g., *I never saw a yellow goat. / I never hope to see one. / But I can tell you, and I quote, / I'd rather see than be one.* Have children illustrate their poems and then compile their creations into a class book.

I Raised a Great Hullabaloo

I raised a great hullabaloo

When I found a large mouse in my stew.

Said the waiter, "Don't shout

And wave it all about,

Or the rest will be wanting one, too."

© 2019 by Irene C. Fountas and Gay Su Pinnell from *Sing a Song of Poetry, Grade 2*. Portsmouth, NH: Heinemann. May be photocopied for classroom use only.

SUGGESTION: This is a limerick that begs to be acted out. Have children take turns sitting in front of a bowl or paper cup and pulling out a large paper mouse. To add variation, invite them to change the food, the unsavory thing found in the food, the person who addresses the narrator, as well as the final line's end-rhyme if children wish to find a synonym for *hullabaloo* (*brouhaha, fuss, commotion, racket*, etc.). For example: *I raised a great commotion / When I found a frog in my potion. / Said the witch, "Don't shout, / And wave it all about, / Or the rest will share your emotion."*

I Saw Esau

I saw Esau sawing wood,

And Esau saw I saw him.

Though Esau saw I saw him saw,

Still Esau went on sawing!

SUGGESTION: This is a tricky tongue twister. Have children think about which syllables or words to stress and which to run together to convey the correct meaning. Ask them to pause after the first line, read the second line quickly, pause after the third line, and then read the last line quickly. A printed copy will help children to read and practice at their own pace.

I Thought

I thought a thought.

But the thought I thought

Wasn't the thought I thought I thought.

If the thought I thought I thought,

Had been the thought I thought,

I wouldn't have thought so much.

SUGGESTION: Children will want to ponder the meaning of each line, noticing how *thought* can be a noun and a verb. Also, stringing *I thought* together adds to and changes the meaning. Invite children to add more lines to the poem, playing with words in the same way.

fold here

I Went to the Pictures Tomorrow

I went to the pictures tomorrow,

I took a front seat at the back.

I fell from the pit to the gallery,

And broke a front bone in my back.

A lady she gave me some chocolate,

I ate it and gave it her back.

I phoned for a taxi and walked it,

And that's why I never came back.

SUGGESTION: This nonsense poem is full of contrasts. While reciting it as a class, make a chart listing the contrasting words. Illustrating each line may also help children decipher the impossible. For example, drawing a calendar with today and tomorrow's date will help them visualize why it's too early to enjoy a movie on a day that has not yet come to pass.

If All the Little Raindrops

If all the little raindrops
Were lemon drops and gumdrops
Oh, what a rain that would be!
Standing outside with my mouth open wide
Ah, ah, ah, ah, ah, ah, ah, ah, ah, ah
If all the raindrops
Were lemon drops and gumdrops
Oh, what a rain that would be!

If all the little snowflakes
Were candy bars and milkshakes
Oh, what a snow that would be!
Standing outside with my mouth open wide
Ah, ah, ah, ah, ah, ah, ah, ah, ah, ah
If all the snowflakes
Were candy bars and milkshakes
Oh, what a snow that would be!

If all the little sunbeams
Were bubblegum and ice cream
Oh, what a sun that would be!
Standing outside with my mouth open wide
Ah, ah, ah, ah, ah, ah, ah, ah, ah, ah
If all the sunbeams
Were bubblegum and ice cream
Oh, what a sun that would be!

SUGGESTION: Invite children to pretend to catch the sweets on their tongues as they say *ah*. After they are familiar with the poem, have children substitute other favorite foods that rhyme with *raindrops, snowflakes,* and *sunbeams.* Alternative weather words can be used as well. Pair this poem with the picture book *Cloudy With a Chance of Meatballs* by Judi Barrett (1978) found in the *Fountas & Pinnell Classroom™ Interactive Read-Aloud Collection, Grade 2* (2018).

fold here

If All the Seas Were One Sea

If all the seas were one sea,

What a great sea it would be!

And if all the trees were one tree,

What a great tree it would be!

And if all the axes were one axe,

What a great axe it would be!

And if all the men were one man,

What a great man he would be!

And if the great man took the great axe

And cut down the great tree

And let it fall into the great sea,

What a great splish-splash that would be!

SUGGESTION: To perform this poem, divide the class into two groups. Ask one group to read the *if* lines and the other to read the lines beginning with *What*. Then have the whole class read the last line—reciting *great splish-splash* with enthusiasm. Refer to this poem when studying the formation of plurals.

If All the World Were Apple Pie

If all the world were apple pie,

And all the sea were ink,

If all the trees

Were bread and cheese,

What should we have to drink?

fold here

SUGGESTION: This poem juxtaposes strange ideas that children will like to imagine. Invite them to talk about how imagination and nonsense are used to make the poem interesting. Then ask children to think of their own silly, creative ideas.

If Wishes Were Horses

If wishes were horses,

Beggars would ride;

If turnips were watches,

I would wear one by my side.

SUGGESTION: Children may find it intriguing to discuss the meaning of these two expressions. Ask them if they know any other sayings. Then invite the class to create new expressions using the poem's *If _____ were_____* pattern.

If You Ever

If you ever, ever, ever

Meet a grizzly bear,

You will never, never, never

Meet another grizzly bear.

If you ever, ever, ever,

If you ever meet a whale,

You must never, never, never,

You must never touch its tail,

For if you ever, ever, ever,

If you ever touch its tail,

You will never, never, never

Meet another whale.

SUGGESTION: Children will enjoy the joke about why they will never meet another grizzly bear (or whale) if they meet just one. Invite them to create their own *If you ever . . . / You will never . . .* verses alone or in groups. Patterns like this help children understand language and give them predictable structures on which to build.

fold here

If You Notice

If you noticed this notice,

You will notice

That this notice

Is not worth noticing.

fold here

SUGGESTION: Invite children to talk about what makes this poem humorous. Also, draw attention to the different uses of *notice* (as a verb, noun, and gerund). Then ask children to create their own poems by picking a new multi-use, multi-meaning word. For example, *If you show this show, / You will show / That this show / Is not worth showing.*

I'm a Frozen Icicle

I'm a frozen icicle

Hanging by your door.

When it's cold outside,

I grow even more.

When it's warm outside,

You'll find me on the floor!

© 2019 by Irene C. Fountas and Gay Su Pinnell from *Sing a Song of Poetry, Grade 2*. Portsmouth, NH: Heinemann. May be photocopied for classroom use only.

SUGGESTION: Teach the poem and talk about icicles. Children who have never seen icicles will find them fascinating. Ask the class to talk about the effects that weather has on water.

fold here

In the Morning

This is the way

We brush our teeth

Brush our teeth

Brush our teeth.

This is the way

We brush our teeth

So early in the morning.

SUGGESTION: Most children will know this verse sung to the tune of "The Mulberry Bush." Invite them to create new verses about activities they do throughout the day. The sillier the activity, the better! This is a good song to revisit when working with homonyms. Children can refer to its list of homonyms (*way, brush, so*) to help extend the song. They may also weave in homophones: e.g., *This is the way we ate the eight*; *This is how we know it's no.*

Intery, Mintery, Cutery, Corn

Intery, mintery, cutery, corn,

Apple seed and apple thorn;

Wire, briar, limber lock,

Three geese in a flock.

One flew east,

And one flew west,

And one flew over the cuckoo's nest.

© 2019 by Irene C. Fountas and Gay Su Pinnell from *Sing a Song of Poetry, Grade 2.* Portsmouth, NH: Heinemann. May be photocopied for classroom use only.

fold here

SUGGESTION: Children will enjoy the word *play* in this nonsense poem. Have them chant the first four lines; assign soloists for the final three lines. Then invite children to channel their inner silly selves by writing a class nonsense poem using this one as a model. It may help to make a list on chart paper detailing common features of nonsense writing.

I've Been Working on the Railroad

I've been working on the railroad,
All the live long day,
I've been working on the railroad,
Just to pass the time away.
Don't you hear the whistle blowing?
Rise up so early in the morn.
Don't you hear the captain shouting,
Dinah, blow your horn?

Dinah, won't you blow,
Dinah, won't you blow,
Dinah, won't you blow your horn?
Dinah, won't you blow,
Dinah, won't you blow,
Dinah, won't you blow your horn?

Someone's in the kitchen with Dinah,
Someone's in the kitchen, I know,
Someone's in the kitchen with Dinah
Strumming on the old banjo.

Fee, fie, fiddle-e-i-o
Fee, fie, fiddle-e-i-o-o-o-o.
Fee, fie, fiddle-e-i-o,
Strumming on the old banjo.

SUGGESTION: Children will enjoy this old folk song. Invite them to play simple rhythm instruments while they sing. Children can make banjos out of empty, rectangle tissue boxes and rubber bands.

Jack Frost

Jack Frost bites your nose.

He chills your cheeks and freezes your toes.

He comes every year when winter is here

And stays until spring is near.

SUGGESTION: Teach the class the meaning of *personification*. Jack Frost is the personification of frost or very wintry weather. Children may find it fun to draw and share their own versions of Jack Frost.

fold here

Jack-a-Nory

I'll tell you a story

About Jack-a-Nory,

And now my story's begun;

I'll tell you another

About his brother,

And now my story is done!

fold here

SUGGESTION: Have groups of children read alternate lines. Then ask the whole class to read the final line together. Be sure they acknowledge the exclamation mark by reading with enthusiasm. Discuss the idea of a story poem as well as what makes this particular one humorous.

Jelly on the Plate

Jelly on the plate.

Jelly on the plate.

Wibble, wobble,

Wibble, wobble,

Jelly on the plate.

Pudding in the pan.

Pudding in the pan.

Ooey, gooey,

Ooey, gooey,

Pudding in the pan.

Soup in the pot.

Soup in the pot.

Bubble, bubble,

Bubble, bubble,

Soup in the pot.

continued

fold here

Snowflakes on my nose.

Snowflakes on my nose.

Sniffle, snuffle,

Sniffle, snuffle,

Snowflakes on my nose.

Raindrops in my shoes.

Raindrops in my shoes.

Sloshy, slushy,

Sloshy, slushy,

Raindrops in my shoes.

Cookies on the plate.

Cookies on the plate.

Gobble, gobble,

Gobble, gobble,

Cookies on the plate.

SUGGESTION: While reciting the poem, children will enjoy pantomiming its nonsensical and onomatopoeic words. Teach children that *onomatopoeia* is "a word that looks like the sound it makes." Use examples from the poem when defining *onomatopoeia*. Once children are familiar with the poem's structure, help them to make up new verses. A good strategy is to brainstorm onomatopoeic or nonsensical words as a class, and then invite children to create new verses in small groups or with partners. Children will enjoy presenting their work to the class as well as comparing each group's creations.

John Jacob Jingleheimer Schmidt

John Jacob Jingleheimer Schmidt

His name is my name, too!

Whenever we go out,

The people always shout

"There goes John Jacob Jingleheimer Schmidt!"

Da da da da da da da.

SUGGESTION: This is an old camp song with a surprise ending. Invite children to sing the verse several times, each time with a softer voice. But have them shout *Da da da da da da da* each time they reach the last line. Introduce the class to recorded versions, such as *Drew's Famous Kids Camp Songs* (2003) sung by a variety of artists.

fold here

Kitten Is Hiding

A kitten is hiding under a chair.

I looked and I looked for her everywhere,

Under the table and under the bed.

I looked in the corner, and when I said,

"Come, kitty, come, kitty, here's milk for you,"

Kitty came running, calling, "Mew, mew, mew."

SUGGESTION: Invite children to act out this poem as they recite it. Because all of the words are probably within your children's oral-language vocabulary, this is a good poem to revisit when using word-solving actions to divide words into syllables.

Knock, Knock

"Knock, knock!"

"Who's there?"

"Lettuce."

"Lettuce who?"

"Lettuce in. It's cold out here."

SUGGESTION: Children enjoy the *knock, knock* genre of jokes and will have fun repeating them over and over. Use this poem to illustrate how a *knock, knock* joke plays with words and their sounds. Invite children to make up their own jokes or ask friends and family to tell more of them.

fold here

The Land of Counterpane

by Robert Louis Stevenson

When I was sick and lay a-bed,

I had two pillows at my head,

And all my toys beside me lay

To keep me happy all the day.

And sometimes for an hour or so

I watched my leaden soldiers go,

With different uniforms and drills,

Among the bed-clothes, through the hills.

And sometimes sent my ships in fleets

All up and down among the sheets;

Or brought my trees and houses out,

And planted cities all about.

I was the giant great and still

That sits upon the pillow-hill,

And sees before him dale and plain,

The pleasant land of counterpane.

SUGGESTION: Have children listen to the poem several times as you read it aloud. Then ask them to talk about the meaning of the poem: the writer compares himself to a giant because he is playing with miniature people and ships. Invite children to discuss their own experiences playing with miniature toys or what they do when they are sick and have to stay in bed.

The Land of Nod

by Robert Louis Stevenson

From breakfast on through all the day

At home among my friends I stay,

But every night I go abroad

Afar into the land of Nod.

All by myself I have to go,

With none to tell me what to do—

All alone beside the streams

And up the mountain-sides of dreams.

The strangest things are there for me,

Both things to eat and things to see,

And many frightening sights abroad

Till morning in the land of Nod.

Try as I like to find the way,

I never can get back by day,

Nor can remember plain and clear

The curious music that I hear.

fold here

SUGGESTION: Children will enjoy reading this poem and using their imaginations to describe the land of Nod: e.g., *things to eat, things to see, frightening sights abroad,* and *curious music.* For inspiration, share an excerpt describing Neverland from J. M. Barrie's *Peter and Wendy* (1911). To further help stir inspiration, invite children to share other make-believe places from their favorite stories, movies, TV shows, or video games. Afterwards, ask children to illustrate their versions of the land of Nod.

Little Arabella Miller

Little Arabella Miller

Had a fuzzy caterpillar.

First it crawled upon her mother,

Then upon her baby brother.

She said, "Arabella Miller,

Put away that caterpillar!"

ADDITIONAL VERSE:

Little Arabella Miller

Had a great big green snake.

First it crawled upon her mother,

Then upon her baby brother.

They said, "Arabella Miller,

Put away that great big green snake!"

fold here

SUGGESTION: The repetition of *-er* endings (with /ar/ pronounced like /er/) makes this poem rhythmically enjoyable. Once children are familiar with the poem, call attention to the word endings and shared sounds. Then invite them to create their own adaptations: e.g., *Little Poppy Punkey / Had a purple monkey. / It poked and pinched her father / But not me or any other. / He said, "Poppy Punkey, / Put away that monkey!"*

Little Robin Redbreast

Little Robin Redbreast

Sat upon a rail;

Niddle, noddle went his head,

Wiggle, waggle went his tail.

Little Robin Redbreast

Sat upon a hurdle,

With a pair of speckled legs,

And a green girdle.

SUGGESTION: If children do not know what kind of animal a robin is or what it looks like, show them a photograph. Then invite them to recite the poem while performing it as a finger play. Nonsense words like *niddle, noddle* and *wiggle, waggle* add interest. Ask the class to invent other nonsense words that fit the poem's actions.

fold here

The Littlest Worm

The littlest worm	(The littlest worm)
You ever saw	(You ever saw)
Got stuck inside	(Got stuck inside)
My soda straw.	(My soda straw.)

The littlest worm you ever saw got stuck inside my soda straw.

He said to me	(He said to me)
"Don't take a sip	("Don't take a sip)
'Cause if you do	('Cause if you do)
You'll get real sick."	(You'll get real sick.")

He said to me, "Don't take a sip 'cause if you do, you'll get real sick."

I took a sip	(I took a sip)
And he went down	(And he went down)
Right through my pipe	(Right through my pipe)
He must have drowned.	(He must have drowned.)

I took a sip and he went down, right through my pipe he must have drowned.

continued

fold here

156

He was my pal   (He was my pal)

He was my friend   (He was my friend)

There is no more   (There is no more)

This is the end.   (This is the end.)

He was my pal, he was my friend, there is no more, this is the end.

Now don't you fret   (Now don't you fret)

Now don't you fear   (Now don't you fear)

That little worm   (That little worm)

Had scuba gear.   (Had scuba gear.)

Now don't you fret, now don't you fear, that little worm had scuba gear.

fold here

SUGGESTION: This poem is intended to be performed in "echo" fashion: one group says a line and another repeats it directly after. Do this for the first four lines of each stanza, and then have the whole class say each collective line together. Sing to the tune of "The Prettiest Girl I Ever Saw Was Sipping Cider Through a Straw."

Looking-Glass River

by Robert Louis Stevenson

Smooth it glides upon its travel,
Here a wimple, there a gleam—
O the clean gravel!
O the smooth stream!

Sailing blossoms, silver fishes,
Pave pools as clear as air—
How a child wishes
To live down there!

We can see our colored faces
Floating on the shaken pool
Down in cool places,
Dim and very cool;

Till a wind or water wrinkle,
Dipping marten, plumping trout,
Spreads in a twinkle
And blots all out.

See the rings pursue each other;
All below grows black as night,
Just as if mother
Had blown out the light!

Patience, children, just a minute—
See the spreading circles die;
The stream and all in it
Will clear by-and-by.

SUGGESTION: Explain that the archaic word *looking-glass* means "mirror." If possible on a sunny day, visit an outside water source like a river or pond. Children will see first-hand how water can be a mirror reflecting their faces, the sky, trees, etc. Invite them to drop pebbles into the river or pond to show the descriptions in the poem: *shaken pool, wrinkle[s],* and *rings*. Alternatively, search online for a video that shows how a river reflects and moves. You may need to define words like *marten* and *trout* (kinds of fish) to help children decipher the poem's images.

Make New Friends

Make new friends,

But keep the old.

One is silver,

And the other's gold.

SUGGESTION: What kinds of images do the words *gold* and *silver* bring to mind? Let children discuss why the poet uses these words to describe friendship. Consider (re)visiting the poem "Gold Ships" (also in this volume).

fold here

Michael Finnegan

There was an old man named Michael Finnegan.
He had whiskers on his chinnegan.
They fell out and then grew in again.
Poor old Michael Finnegan,
Begin again.

There was an old man named Michael Finnegan.
He went fishing with a pin again.
Caught a fish and dropped it in again.
Poor old Michael Finnegan,
Begin again.

There was an old man named Michael Finnegan.
He grew fat and then grew thin again.
Then he died and had to begin again.
Poor old Michael Finnegan,
Begin again.

SUGGESTION: The repetition of *-gain* and *-gan* exemplifies word endings that are spelled differently but sound the same—making the rhythmic reading of this poem both enjoyable and memorable. Help children see how repeating patterns (e.g., repeating sounds or saying one or more words together quickly) are used to create rhymes when writing a humorous verse. They will enjoy reciting this poem, especially the part that reads *Begin again*, which playfully directs children to the next stanza.

Milkman, Milkman

Milkman, milkman,

Where have you been?

Buttermilk Channel, up to my chin.

I spilled my milk,

And I spoiled my clothes

And I got a long icicle

Hung from my nose.

SUGGESTION: Have some children read the initial two-line question and the rest read the response. This simple verse is a good one to use when children are identifying long and short vowel sounds in words. Or return to it when looking for examples of adding *-ed* to form past tense.

fold here

Miss Mary Mack

Miss Mary Mack, Mack, Mack

All dressed in black, black, black

With silver buttons, buttons, buttons

All down her back, back, back.

She asked her mother, mother, mother

For fifteen cents, cents, cents

To see the elephants, elephants, elephants

Jump the fence, fence, fence.

They jumped so high, high, high

They touched the sky, sky, sky,

And they didn't come down, down, down

Till the fourth of July, ly, ly.

SUGGESTION: Hand-clapping games are good practice for coordination and rhythm. Invite children to play a clapping game with a partner. Have them clap their partner's palms face front, then their own hands, and then their partner's palms again on the first set of repeated words (*Mack, Mack, Mack*). Then instruct children to cross their arms when they clap their partner's palms on the next three repeated words (*black, black, black*). Have them continue this alternation before clapping thighs for the last repeat: *down, down, down.* Show children the rollicking picture book *Miss Mary Mack* by Mary Ann Hoberman (1998).

Miss Polly Had a Dolly

Miss Polly had a dolly

Who was sick, sick, sick,

So she sent for the doctor

To be quick, quick, quick.

The doctor came

With his bag and hat,

And he knocked at the door

With a rat-a-tat-tat.

He looked at the dolly

And he shook his head,

And he said, "Miss Polly,

Put her straight to bed."

SUGGESTION: Have one child say the doctor's words while the others recite the poem together. Invite the whole class to tap along with the repeated words using rhythm sticks, tambourines, or other simple instruments. After children are familiar with the poem, divide the class into three groups—one for each stanza. Invite each group to illustrate its respective lines, and then put the poem back together into a class poetry book.

fold here

Monday's Child

Monday's child is fair of face,

Tuesday's child is full of grace,

Wednesday's child is full of woe,

Thursday's child has far to go,

Friday's child is loving and giving,

Saturday's child works hard for a living,

But the child born on Sunday

Is bonny and blithe and good and gay.

SUGGESTION: This is an old rhyme about the days of the week. You may need to define its use of archaic language (*bonny, blithe,* and *gay*). Ask children to find out on which day they were born. Children born on the same day of the week can then work together to create a new rhyme for *Monday's child, Tuesday's child,* and so on.

The Months of the Year

by Sara Coleridge

January brings the snow,

Makes our feet and fingers glow.

February brings the rain,

Thaws the frozen lake again.

March brings breezes loud and shrill,

Stirs the dancing daffodil.

April brings the primrose sweet,

Scatters daisies at our feet.

May brings flocks of pretty lambs,

Skipping by their fleecy dams.

June brings tulips, lilies, roses,

Fills the children's hands with posies.

continued

fold here

Hot July brings cooling showers,

Apricots, and gillyflowers.

August brings the sheaves of corn,

Then the harvest home is borne.

Clear September brings blue skies,

Goldenrod, and apple pies.

Fresh October brings the pheasant,

Then to gather nuts is pleasant.

Dull November brings the blast,

Makes the leaves go whirling fast.

Chill December brings the sleet,

Blazing fire, and holiday treat.

SUGGESTION: Assign partners and invite children to read these verses to each other—making sure to alternate months. Or divide the class into twelve groups: one for each month of the year. Ask each group to illustrate its stanza (you may need to define archaic language). Then invite children to line up in calendar order and hold up their group's illustration(s) while the class recites its assigned lines. This is also a good poem to revisit for vowel combinations (*ai, ay, ea, ee, ow*) as well as for recognizing syllables.

The Moon

by Robert Louis Stevenson

The moon has a face like the clock in the hall;

She shines on thieves on the garden wall,

On streets and fields and harbor quays,

And birdies asleep in the forks of the trees.

The squalling cat and the squeaking mouse,

The howling dog by the door of the house,

The bat that lies in bed at noon,

All love to be out by the light of the moon.

But all of the things that belong to the day

Cuddle to sleep to be out of her way;

And flowers and children close their eyes

Till up in the morning the sun shall arise.

SUGGESTION: Archaic or unfamiliar words like *harbor quays* and *squalling* may need explaining. (The poem's rhyme will help children with the pronunciation of the word *quays*. It rhymes with *trees*.) Teach children that *similes* are "comparisons of two unlike things, especially in phrases containing the words *like* or *as*." Invite them to help you create their own similes about the moon or other things in nature.

fold here

Moses Supposes

Moses supposes his toeses are roses,

But Moses supposes erroneously;

For nobody's toeses are posies of roses,

As Moses supposes his toeses to be.

© 2019 by Irene C. Fountas and Gay Su Pinnell from *Sing a Song of Poetry, Grade 2*. Portsmouth, NH: Heinemann. May be photocopied for classroom use only.

fold here

SUGGESTION: Help children hear the playful language sounds as they recite and read the verse. When they are familiar with the language, have children read it more quickly. Refer back to this poem when reviewing /ō/: e.g., *Moses, supposes, toeses,* and *roses.*

A Mouse in Her Room

A mouse in her room woke Miss Dowd,

Who was frightened and screamed very loud.

Then a happy thought hit her—

To scare off the critter,

She sat up in her bed and meowed.

© 2019 by Irene C. Fountas and Gay Su Pinnell from *Sing a Song of Poetry, Grade 2*. Portsmouth, NH: Heinemann. May be photocopied for classroom use only.

SUGGESTION: Invite children to talk about why what Miss Dowd did was so clever. They'll need to think from the mouse's perspective! Then ask the class to replace *mouse* with different animals while also brainstorming new sounds Miss Dowd needs to make to scare the animals away.

fold here

Mr. Crocodile

Three little monkeys swinging from a tree,

Teasing Mr. Crocodile, "You can't catch me!"

Along came Mr. Crocodile, quiet as can be . . . SNAP!

Two little monkeys swinging from a tree,

Teasing Mr. Crocodile, "You can't catch me!"

Along came Mr. Crocodile, quiet as can be . . . SNAP!

One little monkey swinging from a tree,

Teasing Mr. Crocodile, "You can't catch me!"

Along came Mr. Crocodile, quiet as can be . . . SNAP!

"MISSED ME!"

fold here

SUGGESTION: Invite children to recite this poem together as a whole class. On the last line of each stanza, have them make a crocodile's mouth with outstretched arms, slowly opening them up before snapping them shut on *SNAP!* Children can all shout *SNAP!* as well as *MISSED ME!* when it's time to pretend to duck out of the way.

Mr. Nobody

I know a funny little man,
As quiet as a mouse,
Who does the mischief that is done
In everybody's house!

There's no one ever sees his face,
And yet we all agree
That every plate we break was cracked
By Mr. Nobody.

It's he who always tears our books,
Who leaves the door ajar.
He pulls the buttons from our shirts,
And scatters pins afar.

He puts damp wood upon the fire,
That kettles cannot boil;
His are the feet that bring in mud,
And all the carpets soil.

The finger marks upon the door
By none of us are made;
We never leave the blinds unclosed,
To let the curtains fade.

The ink we never spill; the boots
That lying 'round you see
Are not our boots—they all belong
To Mr. Nobody.

SUGGESTION: Children will enjoy—and perhaps relate to—this humorous poem about blaming mischief on a mysterious Mr. Nobody instead of the naughty narrators. Make a list together of all the things for which Mr. Nobody could be responsible. Scribe for the class or let children take turns adding to the list as well as illustrating it. Consider pairing this poem with picture books about mischievous children, like James Marshall's *Miss Nelson Is Missing!* (1977) and *Miss Nelson Is Back* (1982) found in the *Fountas & Pinnell Classroom™ Interactive Read-Aloud Collection, Grade 2* (2018). Read back the list for a shared reading experience.

The Mulberry Bush

Here we go 'round the mulberry bush,

The mulberry bush, the mulberry bush.

Here we go 'round the mulberry bush,

So early in the morning.

ADDITIONAL VERSES:

This is the way we wash our clothes,
Wash our clothes, wash our clothes.
This is the way we wash our clothes,
So early Monday morning.

This is the way we iron our clothes,
Iron our clothes, iron our clothes.
This is the way we iron our clothes,
So early Tuesday morning.

This is the way we mend our clothes,
Mend our clothes, mend our clothes.
This is the way we mend our clothes,
So early Wednesday morning.

This is the way we scrub the floor,
Scrub the floor, scrub the floor.
This is the way we scrub the floor,
So early Thursday morning

This is the way we sweep the house,
Sweep the house, sweep the house.
This is the way we sweep the house,
So early Friday morning.

This is the way we bake our bread,
Bake our bread, bake our bread.
This is the way we bake our bread,
So early Saturday morning.

This is the way we walk the dog,
Walk the dog, walk the dog.
This is the way we walk the dog,
So early Sunday morning.

fold here

SUGGESTION: Children enjoy singing this song and pantomiming its actions. Once they are familiar with the poem's pattern and structure, invite them to invent their own verses: e.g., *This is the way we ride our bikes, This is the way we play in the park*, and so on.

My Bed Is a Boat

by Robert Louis Stevenson

My bed is like a little boat;
Nurse helps me in when I embark;
She girds me in my sailor's coat
And starts me in the dark.

At night I go on board and say
Good-night to all my friends on shore;
I shut my eyes and sail away
And see and hear no more.

And sometimes things to bed I take,
As prudent sailors have to do;
Perhaps a slice of wedding-cake,
Perhaps a toy or two.

All night across the dark we steer;
But when the day returns at last,
Safe in my room beside the pier,
I find my vessel fast.

SUGGESTION: Children will relate to the narrator's imaginative play. Invite them to talk about the things they pretend to be—now or when they were younger. Explain how the narrator uses his or her imagination to pretend that the bed is a boat sailing him/her to a land of dreams. Ask children about the things they use(d) for make-believe play: e.g., forts, toys, stuffed animals, dolls, etc. Afterwards, divide children into small groups. Give each group a couple of every-day props to create a pretend scenario: e.g., a few classroom chairs and a whistle can transform into a choo-choo train with a conductor and passengers. Invite children to guess each group's pretend performance.

fold here

My Father Is Extremely Tall

My father is extremely tall

When he stands upright like a wall—

But I am very short and small.

Yet I am growing, so they say,

A little taller every day.

SUGGESTION: Invite children to recite the poem as they act out the idea of being tall and small. Help them see that all measurements are relative; to a mouse we are tall, yet we are very small compared to an elephant. Now have children draw two illustrations, each depicting themselves next to a different-sized animal. Then ask them to label the subjects as either small or tall in each comparative drawing.

My Old Hen

I went down to my garden patch

To see if my old hen had hatched.

She'd hatched out her chickens and the peas were green.

She sat there a-peckin' on a tambourine.

SUGGESTION: Invite children to shake a tambourine while reciting this poem. Then have them talk about how the poem's images are realistic until the last line, at which point the poem transforms into nonsense. Ask them to make up new, fanciful, final lines. Afterwards, have them illustrate their revised versions and then paste them together in a class poetry book.

fold here

My Shadow

by Robert Louis Stevenson

I have a little shadow that goes in and out with me,

And what can be the use of him is more than I can see.

He is very, very like me from the heels up to the head;

And I see him jump before me when I jump into my bed.

The funniest thing about him is the way he likes to grow—

Not at all like proper children, which is always very slow;

For he sometimes shoots up taller like an india-rubber ball,

And he sometimes gets so little that there's none of him at all.

ADDITIONAL VERSES:

He hasn't got a notion of how children ought to play,

And can only make a fool of me in every sort of way.

He stays so close beside me, he's a coward you can see;

I'd think shame to stick to nursie as that shadow sticks to me!

One morning, very early, before the sun was up,

I rose and found the shining dew on every buttercup;

But my lazy little shadow, like an arrant sleepy-head,

Had stayed at home behind me and was fast asleep in bed.

fold here

SUGGESTION: Have children swing back and forth at the beginning of the first verse, stretch tall at the beginning of the second verse, and then curl up at the end. After they are familiar with this poem, invite children to create shadow art. First, ask them to draw a picture of themselves. Next, have them cut out their picture, place it over a black piece of paper, and then cut around it. This will produce two cutout images; the drawing and a black shadow. Finally, instruct children to attach both cutouts to paper, with feet touching, to create a real shadow picture.

Nest Eggs

by Robert Louis Stevenson

Here in the fork

The brown nest is seated;

Four little blue eggs

The mother keeps heated.

SUGGESTION: Children may need a little help puzzling out this poem. Have them brainstorm the meaning of *fork* in this context (tree fork), and discuss how and why the mother bird heats the eggs. Pair this playful poem with a nonfiction book about birds or nests, such as *About Birds: A Guide for Children* by Cathryn Sill (1991).

fold here

New Shoes

My shoes are new and squeaky shoes,

They're shiny, creaky shoes,

I wish I had my leaky shoes

That my mother threw away.

I liked my old brown leaky shoes,

Much better than these creaky shoes,

These shiny, creaky, squeaky shoes

I've got to wear today.

fold here

SUGGESTION: Children will relate to the idea that well-worn shoes might be more comfortable than new shoes. Hand out photocopies of this poem and invite children to illustrate old and new shoes. Consider asking the class to brainstorm other things they do not prefer brand new.

New Sights

I like to see a thing I know

Has not been seen before,

That's why I cut my apple through

To look into the core.

It's nice to think, though many an eye

Has seen the ruddy skin,

Mine is the very first to spy

The five brown pips within.

SUGGESTION: This poem is about the unknown or unseen hiding in plain view. Invite children to talk about what other seemingly familiar things they can be the first to look at by interacting with them in new ways. Also help them understand that *pips* are "seeds."

fold here

Night

by William Blake

The sun descending in the west,

The evening star does shine;

The birds are silent in their nest,

And I must seek for mine.

The moon, like a flower

In heaven's high bower,

With silent delight

Sits and smiles on the night.

© 2019 by Irene C. Fountas and Gay Su Pinnell from *Sing a Song of Poetry, Grade 2*. Portsmouth, NH: Heinemann. May be photocopied for classroom use only.

SUGGESTION: Children will enjoy talking about the comparisons in this poem: a nest compared to your own bed, the moon to a flower, and heaven to a garden. Point out how the moon is personified. That is, call attention to how the poet writes about the moon as if it is alive. Additional verses to this poem can be found online.

A Nonsense Alphabet

by Edward Lear

A was once an apple pie,
Pidy
Widy
Tidy
Pidy
Nice Insidy
Apple Pie!

B was once a little bear,
Beary
Wary
Hairy
Beary
Taky Cary
Little Bear!

C was once a little cake,
Caky
Baky
Maky
Caky
Taky Caky,
Little Cake!

D was once a little doll,
Dolly
Molly
Polly
Dolly
Nursey Dolly
Little Doll!

E was once a little eel,
Eely
Weely
Peely
Eely
Twirly Tweely
Little Eel!

F was once a little fish,
Fishy
Wishy
Squishy
Fishy
In a Dishy
Little Fish!

continued

fold here

G was once a little goose,
Goosey
Moosey
Boosey
Goosey
Waddly Woosey
Little Goose!

H was once a little hen,
Henny
Chenny
Tenny
Henny
Eggsy Any
Little Hen?

I was once a bottle of ink,
Inky
Dinky
Thinky
Inky
Blacky Minky
Bottle of Ink!

J was once a jar of jam,
Jammy
Mammy
Clammy
Jammy
Sweety Swammy
Jar of Jam!

K was once a little kite,
Kity
Whity
Flighty
Kity
Out of Sighty
Little Kite!

L was once a little lark,
Larky
Marky
Harky
Larky
In the Parky
Little Lark!

continued

fold here

M was once a little mouse,
Mousey
Bousey
Sousey
Mousey
In the Housey
Little Mouse!

N was once a little needle,
Needly
Tweedly
Threedly
Needly
Wisky Wheedly
Little Needle!

O was once a little owl,
Owly
Prowly
Howly
Owly
Browny Fowly
Little Owl!

P was once a little pump,
Pumpy
Slumpy
Flumpy
Pumpy
Dumpy Thumpy
Little Pump!

Q was once a little quail,
Quaily
Faily
Daily
Quaily
Stumpy Taily
Little Quail!

R was once a little rose,
Rosy
Posy
Nosy
Rosy
Blows-y Grows-y
Little Rose!

continued

fold here

S was once a little shrimp,
Shrimpy
Nimpy
Flimpy
Shrimpy
Jumpy Jimpy
Little Shrimp!

T was once a little thrush,
Thrushy
Hushy
Bushy
Thrushy
Flitty Flushy
Little Thrush!

U was once a little urn,
Urny
Burny
Turny
Urny
Bubbly Burny
Little Urn!

V was once a little vine,
Viny
Winy
Twiny
Viny
Twisty Twiny
Little Vine!

W was once a mighty whale,
Whaly
Scaly
Shaly
Whaly
Tumbly Taily
Mighty Whale!

X was once a great king Xerxes,
Xerxy
Perxy
Turxy
Xerxy
Linxy Lurxy
Great King Xerxes!

Y was once a little yew,
Yewdy
Fewdy
Crudy
Yewdy
Growdy Grewdy,
Little Yew!

Z was once a piece of zinc,
Zinky
Winky
Blinky
Zinky
Tinky Minky
Piece of Zinc!

fold here

SUGGESTION: Assign one letter (or more, depending on class size) to each child. Then ask children to illustrate their respective stanzas. Have the class recite the poem aloud in order, according to their assigned letters. Once children are familiar with the poem's word play and pattern, invite them to create their own nonsense alphabet poems.

The North Wind Doth Blow

The north wind doth blow,

And we shall have snow,

And what will the robin do then, poor thing?

He'll sit in the barn,

And keep himself warm,

And hide his head under his wing, poor thing!

fold here

SUGGESTION: To start, explain that the archaic word *doth* means "does." Read the poem aloud, and ask children to pay attention to its mood. Does the robin like winter time? What words and images suggest the robin will not enjoy the *north wind* and *snow*? Instruct the class to read the poem slowly so as to replicate the robin's mood and movement. For a finale, invite children to tuck their heads under their make-believe *wings*.

Now We Are Gathering Nuts in May

Now we are gathering nuts in May,
Nuts in May, nuts in May,
Now we are gathering nuts in May
Out on a frosty morning.

Who will come over for nuts in May,
Nuts in May, nuts in May,
Who will come over for nuts in May
Out on a frosty morning?

Sue will come over for nuts in May,
Nuts in May, nuts in May,
Sue will come over for nuts in May
Out on a frosty morning.

Who will come over to fetch her away,
Fetch her away, fetch her away,
Who will come over to fetch her away
Out on a frosty morning?

Jack will come over to fetch her away,
Fetch her away, fetch her away,
Jack will come over to fetch her away
Out on a frosty morning.

SUGGESTION: Sing this poem to the tune of "The Mulberry Bush." Once children are familiar with the poem's structure, invite them to change the month, what the narrator will do in that month, and the day's description: e.g., *Now we are selling lemonade in July / Lemonade in July, lemonade in July / Now we are selling lemonade in July / On a hot summer morning.* Have children replace *Sue* and *Jack* for classmate's names.

Oh, How Lovely Is the Evening

Oh, how lovely is the evening,

Is the evening,

When the bells are sweetly ringing,

Sweetly ringing,

Ding, dong, ding, dong, ding, dong.

SUGGESTION: Once children know this poem, invite them to use the pattern to create new verses: e.g., *Oh, how tricky is our math time.* Use this song to teach children how to sing a round (a song sung by two or more people in which the first person sings the first line, the second person sings the first line while the first person sings the second line, and so on).

fold here

Old King Cole

Old King Cole was a merry old soul,
And a merry old soul was he.
He called for his pipe,
And he called for his bowl,
And he called for his fiddlers three.

Each fiddler he had a fiddle,
And the fiddles went tweedle-dee.
Oh, there's none so rare as can compare
As King Cole and his fiddlers three.

ADDITIONAL VERSES:

Then he called for his fifers two,
And they puffed and they blew tootle-too.
And King Cole laughed as his glass he quaffed,
And his fifers puffed tootle-too.

Then he called for his drummer boy,
The army's pride and joy.
And the thuds rang out with a loud bang, bang,
The noise of the noisiest toy.

Then he called for his trumpeters four,
Who stood at his own palace door.
And they played trang-a-tang
Whilst the drummer went bang,
And King Cole he called for more.

He called for a man to conduct,
Who into his bed had been tucked,
And he had to get up without bite or sup,
And waggle his stick and conduct.

Old King Cole laughed with glee,
Such rare antics to see.
There never was a man in merry England
Who was half as merry as he.

fold here

SUGGESTION: Children may be familiar with the first verse of this traditional rhyme but perhaps not the rest of the story. This rhyme-song has a lot of rich language with new vocabulary words (*fifers, quaffed, thuds, antics*) and complex language structure. Invite children to create a mural with illustrations for each of the seven stanzas.

The Old Man and the Cow

by Edward Lear

There was an old man who said, "How

Shall I flee from this horrible cow?

I will sit on this stile,

And continue to smile,

Which may soften the heart of that cow."

SUGGESTION: Edward Lear is the master of the limerick, which children enjoy for rhyme and rhythm. Use this poem to help them study limericks (number of lines, which lines rhyme, content) and to talk about what makes them funny. Have children identify the rhyming pattern by asking them to whisper or shout the rhyming words.

fold here

Old Mother Hubbard

Old Mother Hubbard went to the cupboard
To give her poor dog a bone.

But when she got there, the cupboard was bare,
And so the poor dog had none.

She went to the hatter's to buy him a hat.
When she came back he was feeding the cat.

She went to the barber's to buy him a wig.
When she came back he was dancing a jig.

She went to the tailor's to buy him a coat.
When she came back he was riding a goat.

She went to the cobbler's to buy him some shoes.
When she came back he was reading the news.

fold here

SUGGESTION: This is a great story poem about a dog whose owner, Mother Hubbard, goes out to buy him things. Create new verses with the same pattern: e.g., *She went to the cleaner's to get him some clothes. / When she came back he was licking his toes.* Revisit this poem when studying possessives.

On the Bridge

by Kate Greenaway

If I could see a little fish—
That is what I just now wish!
I want to see his great round eyes
Always open in surprise.

I wish a water rat would glide
Slowly to the other side;
Or a dancing spider sit
On the yellow flags a bit.

I think I'll get some stones to throw,
And watch the pretty circles show.
Or shall we sail a flower-boat,
And watch it slowly—slowly float?

That's nice—because you never know
How far away it means to go;
And when tomorrow comes, you see,
It may be in the great wide sea.

SUGGESTION: Invite children to talk about how this poem sets a scene. What details help them feel like they are on the bridge beside the narrator? Now ask children to brainstorm aloud other things they may see or do on or by a bridge. Alternatively, help them create a poem inspired by this one's rhyming scheme. For example, as a class, you might write a poem titled "On the Hill" with lines like: *If I found a little bee / Buzzing all around me, / I would swat and swipe the air / Because its sting I cannot bear! / Or maybe down the hill I'll roll. / Plucking flowers as a goal. / Then hold the petals to the sky / And hope I make an ally.*

fold here

Once I Saw a Bunny

Once I saw a bunny

And a green cabbage head.

"I think I'll have some cabbage,"

The little bunny said.

So he nibbled and he nibbled.

And he pricked his ears to say,

"Now I think it's time

I should be hopping on my way."

SUGGESTION: Some children may have bunnies for pets and may know, for example, why they prick their ears (to listen for scary sounds or predators). Invite children to guess why the bunny in the poem hopped away. Then ask them to talk about other animals' reactions to scary sounds: e.g., a dog may growl, bark, or whimper whereas a cat may hiss or run and hide. Have children pick a new animal and write a poem about it using this one as inspiration. Be sure to also refer to this poem when studying double consonants.

One Bottle of Pop

One bottle of pop in the yard

Two bottles

Three bottles

Four bottles of pop in the yard

Five bottles

Six bottles

Seven bottles of pop in the yard

POP!

Don't throw your junk in my backyard

My backyard

My backyard

Don't throw your junk in my backyard

My backyard's full of POP!

Fish and chips and vinegar

Vinegar

Vinegar

Fish and chips and vinegar

Soda, soda, soda, POP!

SUGGESTION: The primary characteristic of this poem is the rhythm. Have children try out different ways of saying the poem and use rhythm sticks to emphasize the cadences they choose. Make the word POP! sound like a pop or use sound effects instead of saying the word. Depending on your locale, you may need to explain that *pop* is "soda" and vice versa. Also, the *chips* in *fish and chips* are not potato chips; they are French fries.

fold here

One Old Oxford Ox

One old Oxford ox opening oysters.

Two toads totally tired trying to trot to Tisbury.

Three thick thumping tigers taking toast for tea.

Four finicky fishermen fishing for funny fish.

Five frippery Frenchmen foolishly fishing for frogs.

Six sportsmen shooting snipe.

Seven Severn salmon swallowing shrimp.

Eight eminent Englishmen eagerly examining England.

Nine nibbling noblemen nibbling nectarines.

Ten tinkering tinkers tinkering ten tin tinderboxes.

Eleven elephants elegantly equipped.

Twelve typographical topographers typically translating types.

SUGGESTION: This poem depends on the repetition of consonant and vowel sounds. Invite children to notice the patterns in the poem. Much of the vocabulary may be very difficult for them. Define and explain the words they need to know. It may work best as a read-aloud. Take it one line at a time, and have children clap the long words while saying them.

The Orchestra

Oh! We can play on the big bass drum,

And this is the way we do it;

Rub-a-dub, boom, goes the big bass drum,

And this is the way we do it.

Oh! We can play on the violin,

And this is the way we do it;

Zum, zum, zin, says the violin,

Rub-a-dub, boom, goes the big bass drum,

And this is the way we do it.

Oh! We can play on the little flute,

And this is the way we do it;

Tootle, toot, toot, says the little flute,

Zum, zum, zin, goes the violin,

Rub-a-dub, boom, goes the big bass drum,

And this is the way we do it.

SUGGESTION: In this cumulative verse, a new instrument is added, stanza after stanza, to build an orchestra. To help children recall the order, write the words for each instrument noise on a separate paper and assign the noises. As the orchestra grows, have children hold up their noise cards to remind others which comes next.

fold here

Out and In

There were two skunks,

Out and In.

When In was out, Out was in.

One day Out was in,

And In was out.

Their mother,

Who was in with Out,

Wanted In in.

"Bring In in,"

She said to Out.

So Out went out

And brought In in.

"How did you find him

So fast?" asked Mother.

"Instinct," he answered.

SUGGESTION: This poem may be tricky for children at first. It may help to—at first—replace the names In and Out with two names of children in the class. Read it aloud and slowly several times before handing out printed copies. Point out quotation marks and commas so that children will comprehend the meaning of the words. Revisit the poem as you deal with antonyms.

Over in the Meadow

Over in the meadow,
In the sand in the sun
Lived an old mother toadie
And her little toadie one.
"Wink!" said the mother;
"I wink!" said the one,
So they winked and they blinked
In the sand in the sun.

Over in the meadow,
Where the stream runs blue
Lived an old mother fish
And her little fishes two.
"Swim!" said the mother;
"We swim!" said the two,
So they swam and they leaped
Where the stream runs blue.

Over in the meadow,
In a hole in a tree
Lived an old mother bluebird
And her little birdies three.
"Sing!" said the mother;
"We sing!" said the three,
So they sang and were glad
In a hole in the tree.

continued

fold here

Over in the meadow,
In the reeds on the shore
Lived an old mother muskrat
And her little ratties four.
"Dive!" said the mother;
"We dive!" said the four,
So they dived and they burrowed
In the reeds on the shore.

Over in the meadow,
In a snug beehive
Lived a mother honey bee
And her little bees five.
"Buzz!" said the mother;
"We buzz!" said the five,
So they buzzed and they hummed
In the snug beehive.

ADDITIONAL VERSES:

Over in the meadow,
In a nest built of sticks
Lived a black mother crow
And her little crows six.
"Caw!" said the mother;
"We caw!" said the six,
So they cawed and they called
In their nest built of sticks.

Over in the meadow,
By the old mossy gate
Lived a brown mother lizard
And her little lizards eight.
"Bask!" said the mother;
"We bask!" said the eight,
So they basked in the sun
On the old mossy gate.

Over in the meadow,
In a sly little den
Lived a gray mother spider
And her little spiders ten.
"Spin!" said the mother;
"We spin!" said the ten,
So they spun lacy webs
In their sly little den.

Over in the meadow,
Where the grass is so even
Lived a gay mother cricket
And her little crickets seven.
"Chirp!" said the mother;
"We chirp!" said the seven,
So they chirped cheery notes
In the grass soft and even.

Over in the meadow,
Where the quiet pools shine
Lived a green mother frog
And her little froggies nine.
"Croak!" said the mother;
"We croak!" said the nine,
So they croaked and they splashed
Where the quiet pools shine.

SUGGESTION: Children may know this song, but may not have explored all of its verses. Read it aloud together as a class, and ask children to talk about what the poem is describing from stanza to stanza (different animals and their natural habitats). Then invite them to work with a partner to select, learn, illustrate, and read aloud an assigned verse. Collect children's work and reconstruct the poem into a class book. Pair this poem with the nonfiction book *Amazing Nests* by Mary Ebeltoft Reid found in the *Fountas & Pinnell Classroom™ Shared Reading Collection, Grade 2* (2018).

Over the River and Through the Wood

by Lydia Marie Child

Over the river and through the wood,

To grandmother's house we go;

The horse knows the way to carry the sleigh,

Through white and drifted snow.

Over the river and through the wood,

Oh, how the wind does blow!

It stings the toes and bites the nose,

As over the fields we go!

Over the river and through the wood,

Trot fast, my dapple gray!

Spring over the ground like a hunting hound,

For this is Thanksgiving Day!

Over the river and through the wood,

Now grandmother's face I spy!

Hurrah for the fun! Is the pudding done?

Hurrah for the pumpkin pie!

© 2019 by Irene C. Fountas and Gay Su Pinnell from *Sing a Song of Poetry, Grade 2*. Portsmouth, NH: Heinemann. May be photocopied for classroom use only.

SUGGESTION: Teach children this song for the Thanksgiving holiday. Pair it with the picture book *Over the River and Through the Woods* by John Steven Gurney (1992). The illustrations will show children how this holiday was likely celebrated and how people lived in other times and places.

fold here

Owl

A wise old owl lived in an oak,

The more he saw, the less he spoke.

The less he spoke, the more he heard.

Why can't we all be like that wise old bird?

fold here

SUGGESTION: This poem offers readers advice. Ask children to talk about what they think the advice is. Then invite them to write their own advice poems using "Owl" as inspiration. Refer to this poem when studying single-vowel sounds as well as diphthongs (two vowel sounds in a single syllable).

The Owl and the Pussy-cat

by Edward Lear

I
The Owl and the Pussy-cat went to sea
In a beautiful pea-green boat,
They took some honey, and plenty of money,
Wrapped up in a five-pound note.
The Owl looked up to the stars above,
And sang to a small guitar,
"O lovely Pussy! O Pussy, my love,
What a beautiful Pussy you are,
You are,
You are!
What a beautiful Pussy you are!"

II
Pussy said to the Owl, "You elegant fowl!
How charmingly sweet you sing!
O let us be married! too long we have tarried:
But what shall we do for a ring?"
They sailed away, for a year and a day,
To the land where the Bong-Tree grows
And there in a wood a Piggy-wig stood
With a ring at the end of his nose,
His nose,
His nose,
With a ring at the end of his nose.

continued

fold here

III

"Dear Pig, are you willing to sell for one shilling
Your ring?" Said the Piggy, "I will."
So they took it away, and were married next day
By the Turkey who lives on the hill.
They dined on mince, and slices of quince,
Which they ate with a runcible spoon;
And hand in hand, on the edge of the sand,
They danced by the light of the moon,
The moon,
The moon,
They danced by the light of the moon.

SUGGESTION: This classic poem introduces poetry's use of nonsense words (*runcible*)—a favorite style for poets like Edward Lear and Lewis Carroll. It is also a fun poem for children to act out using props made from classroom materials: e.g., a tissue box guitar with yarn to pluck. After props are created and the class is familiar with the poem, assign select children to the four roles: Owl, Pussy-cat, Piggy-wig, and Turkey. Invite each child to recite his or her lines (and/or act out his or her actions) while the rest of the class narrates.

Pairs or Pears

Twelve pairs hanging high,

Twelve knights riding by,

Each knight took a pear,

And yet left a dozen there.

SUGGESTION: Children will enjoy puzzling out this poem's riddle. Consider displaying the poem on chart paper or in a pocket chart to help them compare homophones for meaning. For example, after children differentiate between *pair* and *pear*, ask them to listen to select words in the poem so as to identify their corresponding homophones: e.g., *high/hi*; *knight/night*; *by/bye*; and *there/their*. Finally, divide the class into groups. Hand out a photocopy of the poem to each group, and invite children to create a second verse using other homophone pairings.

fold here

Pawpaw Patch

Where, oh where,
Is dear little Nellie?
Where, oh where,
Is dear little Nellie?
Where, oh where,
Is dear little Nellie?
Way down yonder
In the pawpaw patch.

Come on, boys,
Let's go find her.
Come on, boys,
Let's go find her.
Come on, boys,
Let's go find her.
Way down yonder
In the pawpaw patch.

Picking up pawpaws,
Puttin' 'em in your pocket,
Picking up pawpaws,
Puttin' 'em in your pocket,
Picking up pawpaws,
Puttin' 'em in your pocket,
Way down yonder
In the pawpaw patch.

fold here

SUGGESTION: Children may think that the word *pawpaw* is a nonsense word, but it is actually the name of a tree from central and southern United States that produces oblong, yellowish fruit. Point out the poem's reliance on repetition, alliteration, and dropping of letters so as to replicate dialect. These stylistic literary devices serve the poem's overall rhythmic flow.

Picture-Books in Winter

by Robert Louis Stevenson

Summer fading, winter comes—
Frosty mornings, tingling thumbs,
Window robins, winter rooks,
And the picture story-books.

Water now is turned to stone
Nurse and I can walk upon;
Still we find the flowing brooks
In the picture story-books.

All the pretty things put by
Wait upon the childrens' eye,
Sheep and shepherds, trees and crooks,
In the picture story-books.

We may see how all things are,
Seas and cities, near and far,
And the flying fairies' looks,
In the picture story-books.

How am I to sing your praise,
Happy chimney-corner days,
Sitting safe in nursery nooks,
Reading picture story-books?

SUGGESTION: Invite the class to recite this poem together. Then ask children to talk about why they think the poet writes about picture storybooks in winter. Why in winter and not in spring or summer? It may help to ask this question after only reading the first two stanzas. Then, as a class or in partners, invite children to brainstorm their favorite things to read about and look at in picture storybooks. Are they pretend places and things? Or are they real?

Porridge Is Bubbling

Porridge is bubbling, bubbling hot.

Stir it 'round and 'round in the pot,

The bubbles plip,

The bubbles plop.

It's ready to eat all bubbling hot.

Wake up, children.

Wake up soon.

We'll eat the porridge with a spoon.

SUGGESTION: The poem mimicks the sounds of porridge in the words *bubble*, *plip*, and *plop*. Have children think of other words that sound like a real noise. As part of a shared writing exercise, record the sound words they come up with on chart paper. Or, opt for interactive writing by inviting children to help you record their thoughts. After composing a list, ask them to create their own poems using onomatopoeia: e.g., *The bird is humming, humming proud. / The bee is buzzing, buzzing loud. / Shush says she. / Sigh says I. / Stop humming, buzzing says the crowd. / Shoo, bee. / Flee, bird. / It's quiet time—haven't you heard?*

The Postman

The whistling postman swings along.

His bag is deep and wide,

And messages from all the world

Are bundled up inside.

The postman's walking up our street.

Soon now he'll ring my bell.

Perhaps there'll be a letter stamped

In Asia. Who can tell?

SUGGESTION: Children enjoy sending and receiving mail. Present this poem when the class has written to someone (or ordered something) and received a reply. Then invite children to talk about whether they have ever received letters. If they could write to anyone in the world, who would they write to? Ask children to write a make-believe letter to the person of their choice.

fold here

The Ptarmigan

The ptarmigan is strange,

As strange as he can be;

Never sits on the ptelephone poles

Or roosts upon a ptree.

And the way he ptakes pto spelling

Is the strangest thing pto me.

© 2019 by Irene C. Fountas and Gay Su Pinnell from *Sing a Song of Poetry, Grade 2*. Portsmouth, NH: Heinemann. May be photocopied for classroom use only.

SUGGESTION: Help children notice the playful spellings—*ptelephone, ptree, ptakes,* and *pto*—that emphasize the weird but correctly spelled word *ptarmigan*. Have them use highlighter tape or yellow crayon to mark these words on their own copies of this poem.

Queen, Queen Caroline

Queen, Queen Caroline,

Dipped her hair in turpentine;

Turpentine made it shine,

Queen, Queen Caroline.

© 2019 by Irene C. Fountas and Gay Su Pinnell from *Sing a Song of Poetry, Grade 2*. Portsmouth, NH: Heinemann. May be photocopied for classroom use only.

SUGGESTION: Be sure to pronounce *Caroline* with a long *i* sound to rhyme with *turpentine*. You may need to explain that *turpentine* takes paint off. It is not be good to use on hair, but saying so makes the poem funny. Refer back to this poem when working with the *i*/consonant/silent *e* pattern.

fold here

Rain

by Robert Louis Stevenson

The rain is raining all around,

It falls on field and tree,

It falls on the umbrellas here,

And on the ships at sea.

SUGGESTION: Read the poem aloud to the class. Afterwards, invite children to make a mural backdrop illustrating the rain coming down in different places around the world or a time they experienced rain. Divide the class into groups based on their illustrative interpretations. Then ask children to recite their rain poems as well as explain their choice of illustration.

River

Runs all day and never walks,

Often murmurs, never talks,

It has a bed but never sleeps,

It has a mouth but never eats.

SUGGESTION: Don't reveal the title of this poem; let children solve the riddle, thereby guessing the poem's title. They may need help defining the word *murmurs*. Pair this poem with the picture book *River Story* by Meredith Hooper (2000) found in the *Fountas & Pinnell Classroom™ Interactive Read-Aloud Collection, Grade 2* (2018).

fold here

Robert Rowley

Robert Rowley rolled a round roll 'round;

A round roll Robert Rowley rolled 'round.

If Robert Rowley rolled a round roll 'round,

Where rolled the round roll Robert Rowley rolled 'round?

SUGGESTION: This tongue twister may be tricky for children. Break down each line with accompanying illustrations to help them interpret and track the order of actions. Most children love the challenge of saying these kinds of poems faster and faster.

Rock-a-bye Baby

Rock-a-bye baby

In the treetop,

When the wind blows,

The cradle will rock.

When the bough breaks,

The cradle will fall,

And down will come baby,

Cradle and all.

© 2019 by Irene C. Fountas and Gay Su Pinnell from *Sing a Song of Poetry, Grade 2*. Portsmouth, NH: Heinemann. May be photocopied for classroom use only.

SUGGESTION: Most children are familiar with this classic poem. It's fun to revisit when introducing word-solving actions such as connecting words that have the same spelling but different meanings and possibly different sounds: e.g., *rock, wind, will, fall,* and *down.*

fold here

The Rooks

by Jane Euphemia Browne

The rooks are building on the trees;
They build there every spring:
"Caw, caw," is all they say,
For none of them can sing.

They're up before the break of day,
And up till late at night;
For they must labour busily
As long as it is light.

And many a crooked stick they bring,
And many a slender twig,
And many a tuft of moss, until
Their nests are round and big.

"Caw, caw!" Oh, what a noise
They make in rainy weather!
Good children always speak by turns,
But rooks all talk together.

fold here

SUGGESTION: Children may need you to explain what a *rook* is (a bird). Show them what it looks like and what its nest looks like. Use this poem to introduce a conversation with children about the different kinds of homes animals build. Invite children to talk about other homes that different animals live in and why. For example, some squirrels live in trees—just like birds—while other squirrels live in burrows underground.

A Sailor Went to Sea

A sailor went to sea, sea, sea

To see what he could see, see, see

But all that he could see, see, see

Was the bottom of the deep blue sea, sea, sea.

SUGGESTION: This nonsense rhyme calls attention to the homonyms *sea* and *see*. Adding simple hand movements for *sea* (hand showing motion of waves) and *see* (hand shading eyes as if blocking sun) helps children distinguish the meaning and spelling differences.

fold here

The Sausage

The sausage is a cunning bird

With feathers long and wavy;

It swims about the frying pan

And makes its nest in gravy.

fold here

SUGGESTION: Don't let children overlook the image of a *sausage bird* swimming around and nesting in a frying pan. Teach them to notice comparisons in which one thing is used to represent another. (This poem does not say directly that a sausage is like a bird, but the comparison is implied.) Ask children to talk about why the poet compares a sausage to a bird.

Seasons

In the spring, leaves are growing,
Green, green leaves are growing.
In the spring, leaves are growing,
Growing in the trees.

In the summer, leaves are rustling,
Yellow leaves are rustling.
In the summer, leaves are rustling,
Rustling in the trees.

In the autumn, leaves are falling,
Brown, brown, leaves are falling.
In the autumn, leaves are falling,
Falling from the trees.

In the winter leaves are sleeping,
Black, black leaves are sleeping.
In the winter, leaves are sleeping,
Sleeping in the grass.

SUGGESTION: This seasonal poem is excellent for choral reading. Divide the class into four groups and have each group read its respective stanza's season. Encourage children to create motions that illustrate the meaning of their assigned stanza.

fold here

The Secret

We have a secret, just we three,

The robin, and I, and the sweet cherry tree;

The bird told the tree, and the tree told me,

And nobody knows it but just us three.

But of course the robin knows it best,

Because he built the—I won't tell the rest;

And laid the four little—somethings—in it;

I'm afraid I shall tell it every minute.

But if the tree and the robin don't peep,

I'll try my best the secret to keep;

Though I know when the little birds fly about

Then the whole secret will be out.

We have a secret, just we three,

The robin, and I, and the sweet cherry tree;

The bird told the tree, and the tree told me,

And nobody knows it but just us three.

fold here

SUGGESTION: It strengthens children's auditory processing when they get the chance to hear a poem first, learn it aurally, and later see it in written form. When they do see the written version, children are pleasantly surprised to find they can read it! When saying the poem as a group, invite them to stop before the last word in each line; have one child read each line's last word to highlight the poem's ending rhymes. Be sure to ask children to guess the poet's secret. Talk to the class about how a poet plants clues in his or her poem: e.g., *the robin … he built the—, laid the four little—somethings—in it,* and *Though I know when the little birds fly about / Then the whole secret will be out.*

Seven Blackbirds in a Tree

Seven blackbirds in a tree,

Count them and see what they be.

One for sorrow,

Two for joy,

Three for a girl,

Four for a boy,

Five for silver,

Six for gold,

Seven for a secret

That's never been told.

SUGGESTION: As a shared writing exercise, have the class create additional lines for eight, nine, ten, eleven, and twelve blackbirds. Be sure to point out the poem's rhyming scheme.

fold here

She Sells Seashells

She sells seashells

On the seashore.

The shells that she sells

Are seashells I'm sure.

So if she sells seashells

On the seashore,

I'm sure that the shells

Are seashore shells.

fold here   **SUGGESTION:** This tongue twister is good emphasis for the /s/ and /sh/ sounds. Invite children to highlight *sh* on their own copies of this poem using yellow crayons or highlighters. Have them use a different color for words beginning with *s*.

Silly Simon

Silly Simon met a pieman,
Going to the fair.
Says Silly Simon to the pieman,
"Let me taste your ware."

Says the pieman to Silly Simon,
"Show me first your penny."
Says Silly Simon to the pieman,
"Indeed I have not any."

Silly Simon went a-fishing,
For to catch a whale.
All the water he had got
Was in his mother's pail.

Silly Simon went to look,
If plums grew on a thistle.
He pricked his fingers very much,
Which made poor Simon whistle.

He went to catch a dicky bird,
And thought he could not fail,
Because he had a little salt,
To put upon its tail.

He went for water with a sieve,
But soon it ran all through;
And now poor Silly Simon
Bids you all adieu.

© 2019 by Irene C. Fountas and Gay Su Pinnell from *Sing a Song of Poetry, Grade 2*. Portsmouth, NH: Heinemann. May be photocopied for classroom use only.

SUGGESTION: Children may be familiar with this fun tongue twister, especially its first two verses. Though verses three, four, five, and six may be a bit more challenging, they will provide word examples for principles children are learning, such as adding *-s*, *-ed*, and *-ing* to form new words (*plums, pricked, fishing*); words with double vowel *oo* (*poor, soon*); or recognizing open syllables (*going, water*).

fold here

Sing Your Way Home

Sing your way home

At the close of the day.

Sing your way home,

Drive the shadows away.

Smile every mile

For wherever you roam

It will brighten your road,

It will lighten your load,

If you sing your way home.

SUGGESTION: Have children discuss how singing sometimes makes you feel better or makes jobs easier to do. Explain that *brighten your road* and *lighten your load* does not mean you see better or carry less. Rather, these sayings are used to express feeling better.

Skip to My Lou

Chorus

Skip, skip, skip to my Lou,
Skip, skip, skip to my Lou,
Skip, skip, skip to my Lou,
Skip to my Lou, my dar-lin'.

Fly's in the buttermilk,
Shoo, fly, shoo,
Fly's in the buttermilk,
Shoo, fly, shoo,
Fly's in the buttermilk,
Shoo, fly, shoo,
Skip to my Lou, my dar-lin'.

Repeat Chorus

Cows in the cornfield,
What'll I do?
Cows in the cornfield,
What'll I do?
Cows in the cornfield,
What'll I do?
Skip to my Lou, my dar-lin'.

Repeat Chorus

continued

© 2019 by Irene C. Fountas and Gay Su Pinnell from *Sing a Song of Poetry, Grade 2*. Portsmouth, NH: Heinemann. May be photocopied for classroom use only.

fold here

There's a little red wagon,
Paint it blue,
There's a little red wagon,
Paint it blue,
There's a little red wagon,
Paint it blue,
Skip to my Lou, my dar-lin'.

Repeat Chorus

Lost my partner,
What'll I do?
Lost my partner,
What'll I do?
Lost my partner,
What'll I do?
Skip to my Lou, my dar-lin'.

Repeat Chorus

I'll find another one,
Prettier than you,
I'll find another one,
Prettier than you,
I'll find another one,
Prettier than you,
Skip to my Lou, my dar-lin'.

Repeat Chorus

continued

fold here

Can't get a red bird,
Blue bird'll do,
Can't get a red bird,
Blue bird'll do,
Can't get a red bird,
Blue bird'll do,
Skip to my Lou, my dar-lin'.

Repeat Chorus

Cat's in the cream jar,
Ooh, ooh, ooh,
Cat's in the cream jar,
Ooh, ooh, ooh,
Cat's in the cream jar,
Ooh, ooh, ooh,
Skip to my Lou, my dar-lin'.

Repeat Chorus

Off to Texas,
Two by two,
Off to Texas,
Two by two,
Off to Texas,
Two by two,
Skip to my Lou, my dar-lin'.

SUGGESTION: This song is a lot of fun to sing and skip to. Invite children to form a circle and hold hands. Each time they sing the chorus, have them alternate the direction of their skipping. Pair this poem with the picture book *Cows in the Kitchen* by June Crebbin (1998).

fold here

Sneeze on Monday

Sneeze on Monday, sneeze for danger;

Sneeze on Tuesday, kiss a stranger;

Sneeze on Wednesday, receive a letter;

Sneeze on Thursday, something better;

Sneeze on Friday, expect sorrow;

Sneeze on Saturday, joy tomorrow.

SUGGESTION: Children will find it interesting to learn that the poem's lines represent old superstitions. Ask them to talk about what we now know about sneezes. After children are familiar with the poem, revisit it to look at *-er* endings or double consonants.

Snow

by Issa

I could eat it!

This snow that falls

So softly, so softly.

SUGGESTION: Children will notice that this poem does not rhyme, as is common to a Haiku. In English, a Haiku follows the 5-7-5 syllable pattern, though this translation of a Japanese poem somewhat differs. Point out the poem's sensory images. Invite children to talk about the softness of the snow. If you live in a cold climate, this is a good poem to place in a window on a snowy day.

fold here

Snowman

I made a little snowman,

I made him big and round.

I made him from a snowball,

I rolled upon the ground.

He has two eyes, a nose, a mouth,

A lovely scarf of red.

He even has some buttons,

And a hat upon his head.

Melt, melt, melt, melt,

Melt, melt, melt, melt.

fold here   **SUGGESTION:** Divide the class into two groups, and have them alternate the reading of lines. Ask children to steadily soften their voices over the final two lines, saying the last *melt* in a whisper. Then invite each child to draw the snowman gradually melting across eight frames until the last frame shows just a puddle and the snowman's eyes. Creating these frames will take planning.

Some One

by Walter de la Mare

Some one came knocking

At my wee, small door;

Some one came knocking,

I'm sure—sure—sure;

I listened, I opened,

I looked to left and right,

But nought there was a-stirring

In the still dark night;

Only the busy beetle

Tap-tapping in the wall,

Only from the forest

The screech-owl's call,

Only the cricket whistling

While the dewdrops fall,

So I know not who came knocking,

At all, at all, at all.

SUGGESTION: Mood is important to the recitation of this poem. Invite children to manipulate their voices so as to convey the mystery, awe, and downright spookiness of a *still dark night*, its eerie sounds, and an unknown someone—or something—lurking out of sight.

fold here

Spread It Thick

Yellow butter, purple jelly, red jam, black bread.

Spread it thick, say it quick!

Yellow butter, purple jelly, red jam, black bread.

Spread it thicker, say it quicker!

Yellow butter, purple jelly, red jam, black bread.

Don't eat with your mouth full!

© 2019 by Irene C. Fountas and Gay Su Pinnell from *Sing a Song of Poetry, Grade 2*. Portsmouth, NH: Heinemann. May be photocopied for classroom use only.

SUGGESTION: Children will enjoy picturing this sandwich. Invite them to substitute other colors for jelly, jam, and bread. Have them also invent new condiments to create their own poetic concoctions.

Spring Is Coming

Spring is coming, spring is coming!

How do you think I know?

I see a flower blooming,

I know it must be so.

Spring is coming, spring is coming!

How do you think I know?

I see a blossom on the tree,

I know it must be so.

SUGGESTION: Brainstorm other signs of spring. Write children's ideas interactively, sharing the marker with your class. Invite your aspiring poets to read their words aloud. Afterwards, help them substitute these words in the third line of each verse: e.g., *I see green grass growing*. It may help to display the poem in a pocket chart so you can easily switch out word cards reflecting children's ideas.

fold here

Stepping Stones

Stepping over stepping stones, one, two, three,

Stepping over stepping stones, come with me.

The river's very fast,

And the river's very wide,

And we'll step across on stepping stones

And reach the other side.

SUGGESTION: Plan to perform this poem outside on a nice day. First, read it aloud until the class is familiar. Then, using chalk, draw the *river* and *stepping stones*. Finally, invite children to step carefully on each stone to cross the river as they recite the poem.

Susie Moriar

This is the story of Susie Moriar.

It started one night as Susie sat by the _____.

The fire was so hot,

Susie jumped in a _____.

The pot was so low,

Susie fell in the _____.

The snow was so white,

Susie stayed there all _____.

The night was so long,

Susie sang a love _____.

The song was so sweet,

Susie ran down the _____.

The street was so brown,

Susie ran through the _____.

The town was so big,

Susie jumped on a _____.

The pig jumped so high,

Susie was thrown into the _____.

She couldn't get higher,

But oh! What a ride

Had Susie _____.

SUGGESTION: Consider displaying this poem on a pocket chart. Have children fill in the missing words by selecting prewritten word cards and placing them accordingly. Alternatively, ask them to guess the missing words (each missing word is found on the following line), write them on a blank word card, and then insert them into the poem appropriately. Afterwards, invite children to help you create a new story about Susie Moriar (or new character) with the same structure.

fold here

The Swing

by Robert Louis Stevenson

How do you like to go up in a swing,

Up in the air so blue?

Oh, I do think it the pleasantest thing

Ever a child can do!

Up in the air and over the wall,

Till I can see so wide,

Rivers and trees and cattle and all

Over the countryside—

Till I look down on the garden green,

Down on the roof so brown—

Up in the air I go flying again,

Up in the air and down!

SUGGESTION: Read this poem aloud as a class before recess. Prompt children to think about all they can see when swinging on the playground. Afterwards, invite them to brainstorm other rides that show an aerial view (you may need to define the word *aerial*): e.g., airplane, helicopter, parachute, spaceship, Ferris wheel, and so forth. Finally, have children pick one kind of aerial view and illustrate it.

Take Me Out to the Ball Game

Take me out to the ball game.

Take me out with the crowd.

Buy me some peanuts and Cracker Jack.

I don't care if I ever get back.

And it's root, root, root for the home team.

If they don't win it's a shame.

For it's one, two, three strikes, "You're out!"

At the old ball game.

SUGGESTION: Children may know this classic ballgame song. Once all are familiar, invite the class to perform it; some children will have acting roles, some reciting roles, and some will have both. Ask one child to be the narrator reciting lines one, two, three, four, six, and eight; one child to be the player who swings a pretend bat and strikes out; one child to be the umpire who shouts and acts out *For it's one, two, three strikes, "You're Out!"*; and the rest of the class to act out and recite the roll of *the crowd* that *root*[s], *root*[s], *root*[s] *for the home team.*

fold here

Taking Off

The airplane taxis down the field

And heads into the breeze,

It lifts its wheels above the ground,

It skims above the trees,

It rises high and higher

Away up toward the sun,

It's just a speck against the sky

—And now it's gone!

fold here

SUGGESTION: Children may be familiar with an airplane's take-off routine, though you may need to define the word *taxis*. Invite the class to recite the poem, first in a slow, whisper and then faster and louder as the airplane takes off. Starting on line six, have children taper back to a whisper as the airplane flies farther away.

Teacher, Teacher

Teacher, teacher, made a mistake.

She sat down on a chocolate cake.

The cake was soft; teacher fell off.

Teacher, teacher, made a mistake.

SUGGESTION: Once children are familiar with this poem, invite them to sit in a circle. Ask each child to recite a new verse (substituting other words for *teacher* and other flavors for *chocolate*) about the classmate sitting next to him or her. For example, Arik recites his adapted verse about Marisol, who is sitting next to him: *Marisol, Marisol, made a mistake. / She sat down on a rainbow cake. / The cake was soft; Marisol fell off. / Marisol, Marisol, made a mistake.*

fold here

Terrific Toes

I have such terrific toes.

I take them with me wherever I goes.

I have such fantastic feet.

No matter what, they still smell sweet.

Toes and feet and feet and toes.

There's nothing else as fine as those.

fold here

SUGGESTION: Invite children to talk about why the poem's second line sounds funny (the poet wrote *goes* instead of *go* in order to rhyme with *toes*). Ask them to compare the spelling of *toes*, *goes*, and *those* and to talk about how these words rhyme even though their rimes differ.

There Was a Bee-eye-ee-eye-ee

There was a bee-eye-ee-eye-ee

Sat on a wall-eye-all-eye-all.

And there it sat-eye-at-eye-at

And that was all-eye-all-eye-all.

Then came a boy-eye-oy-eye-oy

Who had a stick-eye-ick-eye-ick.

And gave that bee-eye-ee-eye-ee

An awful lick-eye-ick-eye-ick.

And so that bee-eye-ee-eye-ee

Began to sting-eye-ing-eye-ing.

And hurt that boy-eye-oy-eye-oy

Like anything-eye-ing-eye-ing!

And then that bee-eye-ee-eye-ee

Gave one big cough-eye-ough-eye-ough.

And one last smile-eye-ile-eye-ile

And he buzzed off-eye-off-eye-off.

fold here

SUGGESTION: When children read this poem's nonsense word patterns, they may feel like they're speaking a new language! Use transparent highlighter tape to emphasize these patterns. Invite children to recite this poem using the echo technique: say a line, pointing to yourself, and then gesture to the class to repeat after you.

There Was a Crooked Man

There was a crooked man

Who walked a crooked mile.

He found a crooked sixpence

Against a crooked stile.

He bought a crooked cat.

Which caught a crooked mouse.

And they all lived together

In a little crooked house.

SUGGESTION: Everything is crooked in this nursery rhyme! Invite children to have fun with the language by substituting *crooked* for descriptive words such as *wicked*. They will love creating all these crooked (and alternative) details for a mural.

There Was a Little Girl

by Henry Wadsworth Longfellow

There was a little girl

Who had a little curl

Right in the middle of her forehead.

When she was good

She was very, very good,

But when she was bad she was horrid.

SUGGESTION: Ask children to share ways they have been good, bad, and horrid (you may need to define the word *horrid*). Invite them to think of other words that mean the same as *horrid*: e.g., *terrible*, *naughty*, and *horrible*.

There Was a Little Turtle

by Rachel Lindsay

There was a little turtle.

He lived in a box.

He swam in a puddle.

He climbed on the rocks.

He snapped at a mosquito.

He snapped at a flea.

He snapped at a minnow.

He snapped at me.

He caught the mosquito.

He caught the flea.

He caught the minnow.

But . . . he didn't catch me!

SUGGESTION: Invite the whole class to read the first verse, have half the class read the second verse, have the other half read the third verse, and then have everyone read the last line. Children love to recite this infectious poem while miming the turtle's motions.

There Was an Old Man of Blackheath

There was an old man of Blackheath

Who sat on his set of false teeth.

Said he, with a start,

"Oh dear, bless my heart!

I've bitten myself underneath!"

SUGGESTION: Ask children to compare this Edward Lear-inspired limerick to actual Edward Lear poems found in this book, like "The Old Man and the Cow" or "There Was an Old Man of Dumbree." After children study a number of limericks, invite them to write their own. Then, consider collecting them all into a class book.

fold here

There Was an Old Man of Dumbree

by Edward Lear

There was an Old Man of Dumbree,

Who taught little Owls to drink Tea;

For he said, "To eat mice

Is not proper or nice,"

That amiable Man of Dumbree.

SUGGESTION: Children will enjoy the distinct nonsense of Edward Lear's limericks; the far-fetched idea of teaching owls to drink tea like people (rather than eat mice) is a humorous one. Once they are familiar with Lear's daft writing style, invite children to create their own silly limericks. Each time the class learns a new Lear limerick, ask them to write their own. The more limericks they read, the more they will write—and the more they can add to a class poetry book or a personal poetry book. Nonsense poems such as these are as fun to illustrate as they are to write.

There Was an Old Man with a Beard

by Edward Lear

There was an Old Man with a beard,

Who said, "It is just as I feared!—

Two Owls and a Hen,

Four Larks and a Wren,

Have all built their nests in my beard!"

SUGGESTION: Children will enjoy acting out this poem as well as illustrating it. Consider having the class create paper props like a beard glued on a craft stick as well as cutout birds and a cutout nest. On cue, invite children to tape the appropriate prop onto their beards while reciting the poem.

fold here

There Was an Old Woman

There was an old woman tossed up in a basket,

Seventeen times as high as the moon.

And where was she going, I couldn't but ask it.

For in her hand she carried a broom.

"Old woman, old woman, old woman," said I,

"Oh whither, oh whither, oh whither so high?"

"To sweep the cobwebs off the sky."

"Shall I go with you?"

"Aye, by and by."

fold here

SUGGESTION: Children will appreciate this poem's imagery: an old woman in the sky sweeping cobwebs. Have them talk about what they think the cobwebs are. Also ask children to guess what *whither* means.

There Was a Small Maiden Named Maggie

There was a small maiden named Maggie,

Whose dog was enormous and shaggy;

The front end of him

Looked vicious and grim—

But the tail end was friendly and waggy.

SUGGESTION: Invite children to create variations of this limerick by finding substitutes for *small, maiden,* and *Maggie.* The dog is the main point of interest; ask children why they think this is so. Then invite them to draw a dog that looks *enormous and shaggy* as well as *vicious* and *friendly*; children will find it difficult to show antonyms like *vicious* and *friendly*. Have them brainstorm other antonyms to nonsensically describe the dog. Are they just as difficult to illustrate?

fold here

There Was a Young Farmer of Leeds

There was a young farmer of Leeds

Who swallowed six packets of seeds.

It soon came to pass

He was covered with grass,

And he couldn't sit down for the weeds.

fold here

SUGGESTION: This limerick has a humorous ending. Invite children to illustrate the poem in a sequence of cartoon panels. Then divide the class into two groups: one to read the lines ending with the *-eed* rime and the other to read the lines ending with the *-ass* rime.

There Was a Young Lad of St. Just

There was a young lad of St. Just

Who ate apple pie till he bust;

It wasn't the fru-it

That caused him to do it,

What finished him off was the crust.

SUGGESTION: This poem follows the familiar limerick structure. Ask children to talk about why the word *fruit* was rewritten as *fru-it* (to make the rhyme work).

fold here

There's a Hole in the Bucket

There's a hole in the bucket, dear Liza, dear Liza,
There's a hole in the bucket, dear Liza, a hole.

Well, fix it, dear Henry, dear Henry, dear Henry,
Well, fix it, dear Henry, dear Henry, fix it.

With what shall I fix it, dear Liza, dear Liza,
With what shall I fix it, dear Liza, with what?

With a straw, dear Henry, dear Henry, dear Henry,
With a straw, dear Henry, dear Henry, with a straw.

But the straw is too long, dear Liza, dear Liza,
But the straw is too long, dear Liza, too long.

Then cut it, dear Henry, dear Henry, dear Henry,
Then cut it, dear Henry, dear Henry, then cut it.

Well, how shall I cut it, dear Liza, dear Liza,
Well, how shall I cut it, dear Liza, well how?

With an axe, dear Henry, dear Henry, dear Henry,
With an axe, dear Henry, dear Henry, with an axe.

But the axe is too dull, dear Liza, dear Liza,
But the axe is too dull, dear Liza, too dull.

Then sharpen it, dear Henry, dear Henry, dear Henry,
Then sharpen it, dear Henry, dear Henry, then sharpen it.

continued

© 2019 by Irene C. Fountas and Gay Su Pinnell from *Sing a Song of Poetry, Grade 2*. Portsmouth, NH: Heinemann. May be photocopied for classroom use only.

On what shall I sharpen it, dear Liza, dear Liza,
On what shall I sharpen it, dear Liza, on what?

On a stone, dear Henry, dear Henry, dear Henry,
On a stone, dear Henry, dear Henry, on a stone.

But the stone is too dry, dear Liza, dear Liza,
But the stone is too dry, dear Liza, too dry.

Then wet it, dear Henry, dear Henry, dear Henry,
Then wet it, dear Henry, dear Henry, then wet it.

With what shall I wet it, dear Liza, dear Liza,
With what shall I wet it, dear Liza, with what?

With water, dear Henry, dear Henry, dear Henry,
With water, dear Henry, dear Henry, with water.

Well, how shall I carry it, dear Liza, dear Liza,
Well, how shall I carry it, dear Liza, well how?

In a bucket, dear Henry, dear Henry, dear Henry,
In a bucket, dear Henry, dear Henry, in a bucket.

BUT THERE'S A HOLE IN THE BUCKET, DEAR LIZA, DEAR LIZA,
THERE'S A HOLE IN THE BUCKET, DEAR LIZA, A HOLE.

© 2019 by Irene C. Fountas and Gay Su Pinnell from *Sing a Song of Poetry*, Grade 2. Portsmouth, NH: Heinemann. May be photocopied for classroom use only.

SUGGESTION: Invite children to sing this song together. As they sing, help them substitute names for *Liza* and *Henry*. Alternatively, invite children to cycle through classmates' names. Pick one child to sing the first stanza. He or she then picks a classmate's name to insert into the first verse. This selected classmate then sings the next stanza—in turn picking a new classmate's name. The pattern continues until the second-to-last verse. To emphasize the ending's irony, have all children shout—rather than sing—the last two lines.

fold here

They That Wash on Monday

They that wash on Monday,

Have all the week to dry.

They that wash on Tuesday,

Are not so much awry.

They that wash on Wednesday,

Are not so much to blame.

They that wash on Thursday,

Wash for very shame.

They that wash on Friday,

Wash in sorry need.

They that wash on Saturday,

Are lazy folk indeed.

SUGGESTION: Partners will enjoy reading this poem together, alternating each pair of lines. If you perform it as a class, ask a soloist to read the days of the week. Children may wonder aloud why the poem is about picking just one day of the week to wash. Ask them to talk about why someone may (have) only wash(ed) once a week.

They Walked the Lane Together

They walked the lane together,

The sky was dotted with stars,

They reached the rails together,

He lifted up the bars.

She neither smiled nor thanked him,

Because she knew not how,

For he was only the farmer's boy

And she was the jersey cow!

SUGGESTION: Cover the last two lines of the poem and have children predict how it will end. Who do they think *she* is? What are *the rails* and *the bars*? After children have time to guess, reveal the answer. Then invite the class to write their own riddle poems.

fold here

A Thunderstorm

Boom, bang, boom, bang,

Rumpety, lumpety, bump!

Zoom, zam, zoom, zam,

Clippity, clappity, clump!

Rustles and bustles

And swishes and zings!

What wonderful sounds

A thunderstorm brings.

SUGGESTION: Ask the class to talk about the words in this poem that make them think of real sounds in a thunderstorm. Then invite children to perform the verse using everyday objects and simple rhythm instruments that mimic the sound of a thunderstorm: e.g., bells, wooden sticks, a xylophone, tambourines, and rain sticks. Pair this poem with "I Hear Thunder" (also found in this volume).

Tree Shadows

All hushed the trees are waiting

On tiptoe for the sight

Of moonrise shedding splendor

Across the dusk of night.

Ah, now the moon is risen,

And lo, without a sound

The trees all write their welcome

Far along the ground!

SUGGESTION: This poem is a good one to use when talking about personification. Trees cannot *wait on tiptoe* or *write their welcome* on the ground the way a person can, but the images presented help the reader imagine the stillness of a tree as its shadow grows on the ground under the moon. After softly and slowly reciting this poem together, help children's comprehension by drawing an accompanying illustration or by showing an image that highly supports the text. Then invite children to help you think of other things in nature (living or nonliving) that can be personified: e.g., the wind sighed and the tree's leaves whispered back. Ask children to draw the personified images you create.

fold here

Tumbling

In jumping and tumbling

We spend the whole day,

Till night by arriving

Has finished our play.

What then? One and all,

There's no more to be said,

As we tumbled all day,

So we tumble to bed.

fold here

SUGGESTION: Invite children to make tumbling and jumping hand motions while reciting this poem. Have them read and perform the last line very slowly to imitate tired children as they *tumble to bed*.

The Turtle

The turtle crawls on the ground

And makes a loud rustling sound.

He carries his house wherever he goes,

And when he is scared,

He pulls in his nose and covers his toes!

SUGGESTION: As children recite and read the poem, invite them to stretch out the words slowly, imitating a turtle's movement. To capture the alarm of the last line, have children read it quickly and loudly. Ask the class how the poem's recitation might change if its main character was a different animal: e.g., a rabbit, a hyena, or an owl.

fold here

The Tutor

A tutor who tooted the flute

Tried to tutor two tooters to toot.

Said the two to the tutor,

"Is it harder to toot, or

To tutor two tooters to toot?"

SUGGESTION: The words to this tongue twister are almost musical. Children love to *toot* their way through the poem using a kazoo. Invite half the class to *toot* quietly while the rest recite. Then ask the two groups to switch roles and perform the poem again.

A Twister of Twists

A twister of twists once twisted a twist.

The twist that he twisted was a three-twisted twist;

If in twisting the twist, one twist should untwist,

The untwisted twist would untwist the twist.

SUGGESTION: This challenging tongue twister will help children develop articulation. Read the verse aloud to the class so children can first listen. Then invite them to join in, reading the poem together slowly, until children are comfortable reciting it at a faster rate.

fold here

Two in the Middle

Two in the middle and two at the end,

Each is a sister and each is a friend.

A penny to save and a penny to spend,

Two in the middle and two at the end.

fold here

SUGGESTION: This poem has a contagious rhythm. Invite children to illustrate it—piecing the poem together line after line. It may help them to label their illustrations according to the clues. Alternatively, ask select children to act as models while the class works together to puzzle out the poem.

Two Little Feet

Two little feet go tap, tap, tap.

Two little hands go clap, clap, clap.

A quiet little leap up from my chair.

Two little arms reach up in the air.

Two little feet go jump, jump, jump.

Two little fists go thump, thump, thump.

One little body goes round, round, round.

And one little child sits quietly down.

SUGGESTION: Recite this repetitive and engaging transition poem while children move from one activity to another, or as a signal for gathering on the rug. Notice that this verse provides two examples of words in which the letter *y* makes a vowel sound. Revisit the poem when children are working with that principle.

fold here

Two Little Kittens

Two little kittens, one stormy night,
Began to quarrel and then to fight.
One had a mouse, the other had none,
And that's the way the quarrel's begun.

"I'll have that mouse," said the biggest cat.
"You'll have that mouse? We'll see about that!"
"I *will* have that mouse," said the eldest son.
"You *shan't* have the mouse," said the little one.

I told you before 'twas a stormy night,
When these two little kittens began to fight.
The old woman seized her sweeping broom,
And swept the two kittens right out of the room.

The ground was covered with frost and snow,
And the two little kittens had nowhere to go.
So they laid them down on the mat at the door,
While the old woman finished sweeping the floor.

Then they crept in, as quiet as mice,
All wet with the snow and as cold as ice.
For they found it was better, that stormy night,
To lie down and sleep than to quarrel and fight.

SUGGESTION: When children are familiar with this poem, they will be able to read it easily from a pocket chart, computer projection, or poetry chart. Invite them to act out the parts of the *biggest cat*, *the little one*, and *the old woman*. If needed, define archaic or unfamiliar words like *quarrel*, *shan't*, and *t'was*. Children may also wonder about the contraction *quarrel's* (*quarrel has*). Ask them to guess what it stands for before providing the answer.

Two Times Table

Twice one is two,
Violets white and blue.

Twice two is four,
Sunflowers at the door.

Twice three is six,
Sweet peas on their sticks.

Twice four is eight,
Poppies at the gate.

Twice five is ten,
Pansies bloom again.

ADDITIONAL VERSES:

Twice six is twelve,
Pinks for those who delve.

Twice seven is fourteen,
Flowers of the runner bean.

Twice eight is sixteen,
Clinging ivy ever green.

Twice nine is eighteen,
Purple thistles to be seen.

Twice ten is twenty,
Hollyhocks in plenty.

Twice eleven is twenty-two,
Daisies wet with morning dew.

Twice twelve is twenty-four,
Roses . . . who could ask for more.

© 2019 by Irene C. Fountas and Gay Su Pinnell from *Sing a Song of Poetry, Grade 2*. Portsmouth, NH: Heinemann. May be photocopied for classroom use only.

SUGGESTION: This poem focuses on multiplying by two, so you will not want to use it until you are teaching children multiplication. For each number, flowers or plants are mentioned in the stanza's second line. Have the class read the poem but also look at each mathematical equation. Then invite children to create drawings that represent the answers to the equations.

fold here

Walk Fast

Walk fast in snow,

In frost walk slow,

And still as you go,

Tread on your toe.

When frost and snow are both together,

Sit by the fire and spare shoe leather.

SUGGESTION: Invite the class to talk about walking in winter weather. If you live in a cold climate, children may know how hard on boots and shoes snow, ice, frost, or rain can be. Ask them to discuss the poem's message: stay indoors during really cold weather!

A Walk One Day

When I went out for a walk one day

My head fell off and rolled away,

And when I saw that it was gone,

I picked it up and put it on.

When I went out into the street

Someone shouted, "Look at your feet."

I looked at them and sadly said,

"I've left them both asleep in bed."

SUGGESTION: After children learn this poem, invite them to present it as a play. Alternatively, divide the class into two groups: one to recite each line and another to echo the first group, line after line, in eerie whispers.

fold here

Walking Through the Jungle

Walking through the jungle,
What do you see?
Can you hear a noise?
What could it be?

Ah well, I think it is a snake, Sss! Sss! Sss!
I think it is a snake, Sss! Sss! Sss!
I think it is a snake, Sss! Sss! Sss!
Looking for his tea.

Walking through the jungle,
What do you see?
Can you hear a noise?
What could it be?

Ah well, I think it is a tiger, Roar! Roar! Roar!
I think it is a tiger, Roar! Roar! Roar!
I think it is a tiger, Roar! Roar! Roar!
Looking for his tea.

Walking through the jungle,
What do you see?
Can you hear a noise?
What could it be?

Ah well, I think it is a crocodile, Snap! Snap! Snap!
I think it is a crocodile, Snap! Snap! Snap!
I think it is a crocodile, Snap! Snap! Snap!
Looking for his tea.
HOPE IT ISN'T ME!

SUGGESTION: After children are familiar with the poem's words and structure (a pocket chart version is helpful), ask them to come up with other animals and sounds to create new verses. Consider pairing this poem with Judith Kerr's picture book *The Tiger Who Came to Tea* (1968).

Wash the Dishes

Wash the dishes,

Wipe the dishes,

Ring the bell for tea.

Three good wishes,

Three good kisses,

I will give to thee.

SUGGESTION: Children love to mime the actions and numbers given in the lines of this verse. Its simple structure and examples make it perfect to revisit when working on forming plurals by adding *-es* to words.

fold here

When I Was One

When I was one I ate a bun
The day I went to sea;
I jumped aboard a sailing ship
And the captain said to me:
"We're going this way, that way,
Forward and backward, over the deep blue sea.
A bright yellow sun and lots of fun
And that's the life for me."

When I was two I buckled my shoe
The day I went to sea;
I jumped aboard a sailing ship
And the captain said to me:
"We're going this way, that way,
Forward and backward, over the deep blue sea.
A bright yellow sun and lots of fun
And that's the life for me."

ADDITIONAL VERSES:

When I was three I hurt my knee . . .

When I was four I fell on the floor . . .

When I was five I learned to dive . . .

When I was six the sail I did fix . . .

fold here

SUGGESTION: This poem has the rhythm of a sailor's *chantey*, which is "a song sung by sailors in rhythm to their work." Tell children about the days sailors sang chanteys when working on tall clipper ships. As they recite the poem, invite children to sway like ocean waves, forward and backward, while you, the captain, directs.

Where Go the Boats?

by Robert Louis Stevenson

Dark brown is the river,
Golden is the sand.
It flows along forever,
With trees on either hand.

Green leaves a-floating,
Castles of the foam,
Boats of mine a-boating—
Where will all come home?

On goes the river
And out past the mill,
Away down the valley,
Away down the hill.

Away down the river,
A hundred miles or more,
Other little children
Shall bring my boats ashore.

SUGGESTION: Read this poem aloud several times to emphasize the poetic language. Then rewrite it as a class book or individual booklet, reserving one page per stanza. Because the poem provides examples of vowel combinations (*ay, oa, ee, ea, ow*), use it when children are working on recognizing and using letter combinations that represent long vowel sounds. Also, consider pairing this poem with the picture book *Where Go the Boats: Play-Poems of Robert Louis Stevenson*, which culls four classic verses from Robert Louis Stevenson's *A Child's Garden of Verses, 1885* and is illustrated by Max Grover.

fold here

Whether the Weather

Whether the weather be fine

Or whether the weather be not.

Whether the weather be cold

Or whether the weather be hot.

We'll weather the weather

Whether we like it or not!

fold here

SUGGESTION: Help children talk about the double meaning of *weather* in this poem. After they are familiar with the poem, contrast the words *whether* and *weather,* which in some parts of the United States are pronounced exactly alike and in other parts sound different (the *wh* pronounced softly with air blown out and the *w* pronounced harder with no breath).

Whistle

"Whistle, daughter, whistle,

Whistle, daughter, dear."

"I cannot whistle, Mommy,

I cannot whistle clear."

"Whistle, daughter, whistle,

Whistle all around."

"I cannot whistle, Mommy,

I cannot make a sound."

SUGGESTION: Children may be able to whistle. If they are not able to or do not know how, try to teach them. Once children are familiar with the poem, use it to look at vowel pairs such as *au*, *ea*, and *ou*.

fold here

Who Has Seen the Wind?

by Christina Rossetti

Who has seen the wind?

Neither I nor you:

But when the leaves hang trembling

The wind is passing through.

Who has seen the wind?

Neither you nor I:

But when the trees bow down their heads

The wind is passing by.

SUGGESTION: This poem is full of visual images that children can discuss and appreciate. Invite them to enact the wind as they recite the poem; or one group can read aloud while another group performs. Then ask children to brainstorm other ways the wind is seen in how it moves things: e.g., a windmill, a kite, a balloon, and hair.

The Wind Blows High

The wind,

The wind,

The wind blows high.

The rain,

The rain,

Scatters down the sky.

SUGGESTION: Invite children to talk about the images in this poem; do they inform how the poem can be recited and performed? Have children act out the poem using motions like hands high and swooping for the wind and hands moving quickly down to simulate rain. Invite them to say the word *high* in a high-pitched voice and the word *down* in a low voice. Then ask children to create their own poems using other weather words: e.g., *cloud, hail, snow,* and *sun.*

fold here

Wynken, Blynken, and Nod

by Eugene Field

Wynken, Blynken, and Nod one night
Sailed off in a wooden shoe,—
Sailed on a river of crystal light
Into a sea of dew.
"Where are you going, and what do you wish?"
The old moon asked the three.
"We have come to fish for the herring fish
That live in this beautiful sea;
Nets of silver and gold have we!"
Said Wynken,
Blynken,
And Nod.

The old moon laughed and sang a song,
As they rocked in the wooden shoe;
And the wind that sped them all night long
Ruffled the waves of dew.
The little stars were the herring fish
That lived in the beautiful sea.
"Now cast your nets wherever you wish,—
Never afraid are we!"
So cried the stars to the fishermen three,
Wynken,
Blynken,
And Nod.

continued

fold here

All night long their nets they threw
To the stars in the twinkling foam,—
Then down from the skies came the wooden shoe,
Bringing the fishermen home:
'Twas all so pretty a sail, it seemed
As if it could not be;
And some folk thought 'twas a dream they'd dreamed
Of sailing that beautiful sea;
But I shall name you the fishermen three:
Wynken,
Blynken,
And Nod.

Wynken and Blynken are two little eyes,
And Nod is a little head,
And the wooden shoe that sailed the skies
Is a wee one's trundle-bed;
So shut your eyes while Mother sings
Of wonderful sights that be,
And you shall see the beautiful things
As you rock in the misty sea
Where the old shoe rocked the fishermen three:—
Wynken,
Blynken,
And Nod.

© 2019 by Irene C. Fountas and Gay Su Pinnell from *Sing a Song of Poetry, Grade 2*. Portsmouth, NH: Heinemann. May be photocopied for classroom use only.

SUGGESTION: After reading this poem together, you may need to define unknown or archaic language (*dew, 'twas, wee one,* and *trundle-bed*). Children will enjoy discovering that *Wynken, Blynken, Nod,* and the wooden shoe that sailed the skies are not, in fact, who or what they seem to be. Rather, they are imaginative interpretations of something else. *Wynken* sounds like the word *winking* and *Blynken* sounds like the word *blinking.* Given this, it makes sense that *Wynken* and *Blynken* are tired eyes, and that *Nod* is a child's head nodding off, ready for sleep.

fold here

The Zigzag Boy and Girl

I know a little zigzag boy

Who goes this way and that.

He never knows just where he put

His coat or shoes or hat.

I know a little zigzag girl

Who flutters here and there.

She never knows just where to find

Her brush to fix her hair.

If you are not a zigzag child,

You'll have no cause to say

That you forgot, for you will know

Where things are put away.

fold here   **SUGGESTION:** Children will vie to explain and act out the word *zigzag*. Some children wear zigzag parts in their hair. Invite the class to talk about other zigzags found in the home or school environment.

References

Andrews-Goebel, Nancy. © 2002. *The Pot That Juan Built*. New York, NY: Lee & Low Books.

From *Fountas & Pinnell Classroom™ Interactive Read-Aloud Collection, Kindergarten*. © 2018 by Irene C. Fountas and Gay Su Pinnell. Portsmouth, NH: Heinemann.

Barrett, Judi. © 1978. *Cloudy With a Chance of Meatballs*. New York, NY: Atheneum Books for Young Readers, an imprint of Simon & Schuster Children's Publishing Division. From *Fountas & Pinnell Classroom™ Interactive Read-Aloud Collection, Kindergarten*. © 2018 by Irene C. Fountas and Gay Su Pinnell. Portsmouth, NH: Heinemann.

Brett, Jan. © 1994. *Town Mouse, Country Mouse*. New York, NY: Puffin Books, an imprint of Penguin Young Readers Group, a division of Penguin Random House. From *Fountas & Pinnell Classroom™ Interactive Read-Aloud Collection, Kindergarten*. © 2018 by Irene C. Fountas and Gay Su Pinnell. Portsmouth, NH: Heinemann.

Fountas, Irene C. and Gay Su Pinnell. © 2018. *Fountas & Pinnell Classroom™ Interactive Read-Aloud Collection, Kindergarten*. Portsmouth, NH: Heinemann.

———. © 2018. *Fountas & Pinnell Classroom™ Shared Reading Collection, Kindergarten*. Portsmouth, NH: Heinemann.

———. © 2018. *Fountas & Pinnell Phonics, Spelling, and Word Study Lessons, Kindergarten*. Portsmouth, NH: Heinemann.

———. © 2017. *Guided Reading: Responsive Teaching Across the Grades*, Second Edition. Portsmouth, NH: Heinemann.

Gibbons, Gail. © 1997. *The Honey Makers*. New York, NY: HarperCollins Children's Books, a division of HarperCollins Publishers. From *Fountas & Pinnell Classroom™ Interactive Read-Aloud Collection, Kindergarten*. © 2018 by Irene C. Fountas and Gay Su Pinnell. Portsmouth, NH: Heinemann.

Glaser, Linda. © 2000. *Our Big Home: An Earth Poem*. Minneapolis, MN: Millbrook Press, a division of Lerner Publishing Group. From *Fountas & Pinnell Classroom™ Interactive Read-Aloud Collection, Kindergarten*. © 2018 by Irene C. Fountas and Gay Su Pinnell. Portsmouth, NH: Heinemann.

Hooper, Meredith. © 2000. *River Story*. Somerville, MA: Candlewick Press. From *Fountas & Pinnell Classroom™ Interactive Read-Aloud Collection, Kindergarten*. © 2018 by Irene C. Fountas and Gay Su Pinnell. Portsmouth, NH: Heinemann.

Karas, G. Brian. © 2005. *On Earth*. New York, NY: Puffin Books, an imprint of Penguin Young Readers Group, a division of Penguin Random House. From *Fountas & Pinnell Classroom™ Interactive Read-Aloud Collection, Kindergarten*. © 2018 by Irene C. Fountas and Gay Su Pinnell. Portsmouth, NH: Heinemann.

Knowles, Sheena. © 1996. *Edwina the Emu*. New York, NY: HarperCollins Children's Books, a division of HarperCollins Publishers. From *Fountas & Pinnell Classroom™ Interactive Read-Aloud Collection, Kindergarten*. © 2018 by Irene C. Fountas and Gay Su Pinnell. Portsmouth, NH: Heinemann.

Knowles, Sheena. © 1988. *Edward the Emu*. New York, NY: HarperCollins Children's Books, a division of HarperCollins Publishers. From *Fountas & Pinnell Classroom™ Interactive Read-Aloud Collection, Kindergarten*. © 2018 by Irene C. Fountas and Gay Su Pinnell. Portsmouth, NH: Heinemann.

Marshall, James. © 1982. *Miss Nelson Is Back*. New York, NY: Houghton Mifflin Harcourt Books for Young Readers, an imprint of Houghton Mifflin Harcourt Books for Young Readers Division, Houghton Mifflin Harcourt. From *Fountas & Pinnell Classroom™ Interactive Read-Aloud Collection, Kindergarten*. © 2018 by Irene C. Fountas and Gay Su Pinnell. Portsmouth, NH: Heinemann.

——. © 1977. *Miss Nelson Is Missing!*. New York, NY: Houghton Mifflin Harcourt Books for Young Readers, an imprint of Houghton Mifflin Harcourt Books for Young Readers Division, Houghton Mifflin Harcourt. From *Fountas & Pinnell Classroom™ Interactive Read-Aloud Collection, Kindergarten*. © 2018 by Irene C. Fountas and Gay Su Pinnell. Portsmouth, NH: Heinemann.

McCarrier, Andrea, Gay Su Pinnell, and Irene C. Fountas. © 2000. *Interactive Writing: How Language and Literacy Come Together, K–2*. Portsmouth, NH: Heinemann.

Pinnell, Gay Su and Irene C. Fountas. © 1998. *Word Matters: Teaching Phonics and Spelling in the Reading/Writing Classroom*. Portsmouth, NH: Heinemann.

Reed-Jones, Carol. © 2000. *Salmon Stream*. Nevada City, CA: Dawn Publications. From *Fountas & Pinnell Classroom™ Interactive Read-Aloud Collection, Kindergarten*. © 2018 by Irene C. Fountas and Gay Su Pinnell. Portsmouth, NH: Heinemann.

Reid, Mary Ebeltoft. *Amazing Nests*. From *Fountas & Pinnell Classroom™ Shared Reading Collection, Kindergarten*. © 2018 by Irene C. Fountas and Gay Su Pinnell. Portsmouth, NH: Heinemann.

Schwartz, June. *From Flower to Honey*. From *Fountas & Pinnell Classroom™ Shared Reading Collection, Kindergarten*. © 2018 by Irene C. Fountas and Gay Su Pinnell. Portsmouth, NH: Heinemann.

Schwartz, June. *Weather Watch: Rita's Journal*. From *Fountas & Pinnell Classroom™ Shared Reading Collection, Kindergarten*. © 2018 by Irene C. Fountas and Gay Su Pinnell. Portsmouth, NH: Heinemann.

Shields, Carol Diggory. © 2002. *The Buggliest Bug*. Somerville, MA: Candlewick Press. From *Fountas & Pinnell Classroom™ Interactive Read-Aloud Collection, Kindergarten*. © 2018 by Irene C. Fountas and Gay Su Pinnell. Portsmouth, NH: Heinemann.